CHINA

NORTH VIETNAM

HANOI

BURMA

LAOS

Gulf of Tonkin

VIENTIANE

Udorn

Nakhon
Phanom

Phu Bai

Da Nang

THAILAND

Ubon

Chu Lai

Takhli

SOUTH

Korat

Phu Cat

Pleiku

Qui Nhon

Don Muang
BANGKOK

U-Tapao

CAMBODIA

Tuy Hoa

VIETNAM

Nha Trang
Cam Ranh Bay

PHNOM
PENH

Tan Son
Nhut

Phan Rang

Bien Hoa

SAIGON

Gulf of Thailand

Southeast Asia

★ National Capital

● Principal U.S. Air Base

Binh
Thuy

South China Sea

Thank you to our Department of Defense for
allowing us to reproduce this map for our book.

LESS THAN A HERO
A FIGHT FOR LIFE

A SOLDIER'S STORY OF VIETNAM AND PTSD

RICHIE MONTELEONE
WITH SANDRA CAPUTO

For more information, email lessthanahero@aol.com

ISBN: 979-8-89316-382-7 - E-book
ISBN: 979-8-89316-449-7 - Paperback
ISBN: 979-8-89316-383-4 - Hardcover

Documents in the Appendix Sections at the end
of our book

and

Links for Veterans Help and Contact Information

are also posted on our website.

www.lessthanahero.com

DEDICATION

Dedicated to the men of Company C, 4th of the 23rd Infantry Division. They were the bravest, toughest men I could have ever fought with. They always went into the fight, never ran away from it. They put up with the most difficult circumstances in the jungles of South Vietnam that you could possibly deal with. Always talking about going home to the world, never complaining about their situation. We lived in the worst of conditions. May GOD bless everyone of these men who gave their lives so some of us could come home to what we always referred to as the world. I was one of the lucky ones.

To Herbert T Sherrill, a super guy who saved my life more than once during combat. A big, 6' 2" black dude and a Sergeant E-6. He called me his little buddy. He was killed in combat in June of 1967, leaving a big hole in my heart. I will never forget my big buddy.

CONTENTS

ACKNOWLEDGMENTS

To my wife Kathy, who had to see firsthand what PTSD is like and stood by me through everything. Thanks to all three of my children Chuck, Keith and Nicole. To the therapy dogs I have had in my lifetime, Daisy, Lilly, Rosie and Tulip, who really helped me a lot in times of extreme emotional distress. My parents Nick and Betty, who had to see the worst of me when I first came home and never gave up on me.

To Sandra Caputo for her help with this book, without her writing and computer expertise it would never have happened.

A big thank you to Wholesale Photo of Midland Park, 85 Godwin Ave, Midland Park, NJ 07432. They took the 50 year old slides of my pictures from Vietnam and turned them into high resolution digital files for us.

Thank you to the United States Department of Defense for allowing us to reproduce the Map of Vietnam in our book.

To my Vietnam Veteran friends, Frank Mezzadri, Bill Dillehay and Dennis Reilly who have been such an important part of my civilian life. To my other Vietnam Veteran friends, Sandy Loudis, John Klosterman and George Compton, for helping us with details for this book and helping to organize the photos.

To Jonathan, my therapist from the Vet Center in Bloomfield, NJ, who is also a Combat Veteran, for helping me negotiate a path of forgiveness for all the horrors of war that I had to deal with.

BASE CAMP

It was January 12, 1967. Our group flew in a commercial jet from JFK Airport to San Francisco, then by bus to Travis Air Force Base in California. From there we boarded a cargo jet equipped with seats on the floor for a long flight to Clark Air Force Base in the Philippines, where we refueled. Our destination was Tan Son Nhut Airbase in South Vietnam, very near Saigon. The trip was quite an experience for a 19 year old kid from Teaneck, New Jersey. We landed safely and walked to a small base camp next to the airport that was primarily used to temporarily house incoming and outgoing soldiers. We could hear the sounds of explosions from far away but this place seemed safe. A year later, with the start of the Tet Offensive, this airfield and complex would be regularly bombed and attacked with rockets and small arms fire.

Soldiers at Tan Son Nhut were housed in large tents without sides or screens. This camp was on higher ground, so there was not much of an insect problem, which we did not know anything about yet. Each tent had about twenty cots and a place for us to store our personal belongings. We lined up at an outdoor mess hall for lunch, and while we were on line I slipped and fell into an old water-filled bomb crater. I ate my first lunch in Vietnam in wet clothes. We then relaxed outside or settled into our tents and waited to be called for dinner. We spent that time bullshitting with other soldiers who had recently arrived. A lot of them would not go home.

Everyone already had their orders as far as base camp location, and our group was assigned to Cu Chi Base Camp, about 35 miles north on Highway One. In the morning, they gave us M14 rifles and ammo, and loaded us into the back of an open truck. The ride that day was uneventful. After they dropped us off, the weapons that we had traveled with were taken from us and sent back with other soldiers for the ride back to the airbase. These weapons went back and forth on these same trucks, in the hands of different groups of soldiers, so that they could defend the trucks and the drivers on the road. An armed soldier was always in the cab with the driver. The next morning, each of us was issued a flak vest and helmet to be worn whenever we were outside our camp perimeter. Here is a fellow soldier from that day, posing with his equipment, including his canteen (picture 1). We were also issued firearms and began to understand what life would be like for the next year.

Frank Mezzadri, whom I met when we both reported to our local draft board in Hackensack, New Jersey, was my best friend every step of the way in Vietnam. He would become a friend for life. As of May 2024, he is still alive. During basic training together at Fort Dix, New Jersey, our days started at 4:30am every morning with a run. Then each of us had to enter the mess hall and shout our military ID number as loudly as possible before getting breakfast. Draftees numbers began with US and enlistees with RA. After breakfast it was more physical training including push-ups, sit-ups, jumping jacks and running in place. We had to march and run with a full canteen, an M14 rifle (not loaded) and a military belt. We also had to practice crawling with all that gear, including through and under barbed wire. There would be no barbed wire in Vietnam, our military knew that, but the training was still very valuable as far as dealing with other things in the jungle. We climbed over walls and practiced jumping off ten foot high platforms, learning to fall and roll.

Next was lunch, again shouting out a military ID before eating, and then more running. We practiced throwing non-functioning grenades at sticks in the ground as if it were a game of horseshoes. There was a lot of target practice, and we learned the proper way to fix a bayonet on the end of a rifle. We practiced running at a dummy affixed to a pole, stabbing it in the chest while shouting our ID numbers, and then shouting "kill, kill, kill." We did marching and running while shouting "this is my rifle, this is my gun, this is for fighting, this is for fun." You had to shout your number and present your rifle while shouting "this is my rifle" and then grab your crotch while shouting "this is my gun," then present the rifle again while shouting "this is for fighting" and the crotch again while shouting "this is for fun." That was for exercise only, no one in the Army ever referred to any real weapon as a gun. We learned how to kill with a garrote, a weapon made of two sticks or clubs and a wire, by wrapping the wire around the enemy's neck and twisting the sticks. The end of day and dinner, after shouting your number again before eating, was a relief. This lasted for eight weeks and we learned to sleep standing up.

I took basic training very seriously and got into tremendous shape. I could run a mile in five minutes, thirteen seconds. At the end of this training, there was a contest on who was the best in our group of about sixty men. Whoever came in first would get a three day pass to be used one week before graduation from basic training and I won. The fellow who came in second was Kenny, we were in high school together and both graduated in 1965. He was the quarterback of Teaneck High School Highwaymen Football Team, much taller than me and very athletic. My parents picked me up and I spent those three days with them and with my girlfriend, Gale. We were both immature and still virgins.

Specialized training after basic was called Quartermaster School. Men were sent to different military bases around the country to learn different skills, and most of us also received additional combat training. We had nothing to say about where we were sent or what we were being trained for. I was sent with Frank to Fort Lee, Virginia, and trained to be an armorer. I learned to repair weapons, and my MOS (my job designation) was 76K30. They also gave me clerical training, but Frank had only clerical training the whole time. After Quartermaster School, everyone got a thirty day leave. Again I spent the time with my family and my girlfriend. We were home on leave to get ready for something we did not understand. It wasn't long before I got my orders for Vietnam, and my new friend Frank got the same orders. I packed some personal belongings, my parents dropped me off on Banta Place in Hackensack, and Frank's family dropped him off. A large group of us boarded a bus and headed for JFK Airport. Most of us had never been out of the United States before.

When I arrived at Cu Chi, any clerical positions that I had been trained for were already filled, so they did not know where to assign me right away. Another soldier who arrived with me, Eddie Lowenstein from California, was in the same situation. On base, there was a supply building with several small rooms, one of which was always occupied by the supply sergeant (picture 2). Eddie and I lived in one of the supply building rooms for a few days until both of us received orders to join the 25th Infantry. Eddie would become a lifelong friend. Frank was permanently assigned to our battalion as the mail clerk. Here he is, with mail in his hand (picture 3).

My very first day walking to headquarters to check in, I noticed a soldier from the unit that I was assigned to, sitting on a box. I saw him take out his M16 and shoot himself in the head. Later, I found out that he was supposed to go home the next day.

At first, I wrote nice sounding letters to my parents, telling them that I was a supply clerk stationed at our base camp. I didn't want them or my grandparents to worry about me. I wrote to my girlfriend and lied to her also. In letters to my friend John from high school, I wrote the truth, and although he was home in New Jersey, he seemed to understand what was happening to me. John and I graduated high school together but he went on to college, which meant an automatic deferment. He saw firsthand all the anti-war campus protests, as most college students did then. I was a low level combatant, or a Grunt, as we called ourselves. Our job was simply to go through the jungle on foot or on our APCs and do what had to be done.

Another one of the permanent buildings on base was called the orderly room. It was a large office with communications equipment that was staffed by officers twenty-four hours a day. Records were kept there, and orders came and went through there. I got to know one of the part-time clerks who worked there, John Klosterman, and we kept in touch all these years. He had several other assignments including being a Grunt in our 1st platoon and building bunkers. He helped us with this book, and as of May 2024, he is still alive. Another fellow soldier whom I kept in touch with is George Compton. He was in Company C with me, and was also a squad leader. He was wounded and sent to a hospital in Japan to recover. He helped us with this book, and as of May 2024, he is still alive. On the back wall of the orderly room was a list with the name and rank of all the men that had been killed so far in Company C, 4th of the 23rd. By my sixth month in country there was no more room on the wall, so the adding of names was stopped. It was not only that they had run out of room, they had decided it was too terrible for incoming men to see. So many boys lost their lives and limbs in combat, booby traps, mines and tunnels.

Some Army personnel stationed in Vietnam had jobs at our base camp that did not involve being out in the field or ever being in combat, we called them housecats. The official title for this position is rear-echelon personnel or REMF. They were the very necessary support staff made up of vehicle mechanics, radio mechanics, cooks, clerks and officers behind the scenes. It was said that for each infantry soldier, there were five or six support staff soldiers and officers. For us combat Grunts, we could not help but compare ourselves to them, relatively safe from harm. Only about 20% of the men deployed ever saw combat action. Now, in my 70s, as I travel around the US meeting many Veterans at campgrounds, meetings and gatherings, the ones I meet most often were housecats. Combat Veterans are dying at a much faster rate from the effects of Agent Orange and the stress of PTSD.

In base camp we lived in hooches, large tents that housed about twenty men, and all the doors and windows had very necessary screens. Cu Chi was on lower ground so the insect problem, along with the diseases they carried, was serious. We had showers that were essentially canvas bags hung outside, about two feet by one foot with holes in the bottom. You would pull on a handle for the water to start, wash, and then start the shower again to rinse. All the bathrooms were outhouses with kerosene pots which we would later pull out and burn. We ate in mess halls when we were at base camp. Breakfast could be chipped beef on toast or sometimes pancakes with ham or sausage, not bad. Lunch and dinner was something like roast beef, hot dogs or burgers with a starch and vegetables. I remember thinking that it was probably better than prison food. A few years later, after my discharge, I had the opportunity to experience prison food.

All units were required to keep an orderly, clean hooch and each cot had to be properly made up every morning. Each of us was assigned a permanent place in the hut with a cot and a foot locker, where we stored personal items and some civilian clothes. Even when we were out for weeks at a time, we had this permanent, secure place for our belongings and the same cot. Local Vietnamese women and old men were employed by the Army and worked on our base camp, doing odd jobs like cleaning the outside areas and filling sandbags which we used to build bunkers. Housecats often paid these locals to clean their hooches and do their laundry. Those of us in combat units were usually not in base camp long enough to need those services. Our hooches stayed empty and clean, and we traveled to laundromats in Cu Chi. We were all responsible for our own laundry, including everyday fatigues and civilian clothes. I remember a storefront laundry, owned and operated by a Vietnamese mother and daughter, who treated us well and were happy to have our business. Locals working at our camp had a fondness for gambling, especially our American style poker games. Like everywhere else in Vietnam, many of the women were selling sex.

The hooches that were closest to the perimeter were occupied by infantrymen, and the occupants of those hooches always had to be ready to defend our base camp. Here are two soldiers from my platoon walking near one of the official signs near our perimeter (picture 4). We were near the edge of the Ho Bo Woods, which meant that enemy combatants could easily get close to us without being seen. Enough soldiers were in base camp at any given time, in or near these border hooches, to defend and guard the camp. Sometimes we could see and hear explosions in the distance from inside the camp (picture 5). Other areas of the perimeter were near open roads with bars, roadside shops and houses of prostitution. Those areas were more visible, open and safer. No place was really safe, there was just dangerous and not as dangerous. Here I am, standing in one of those open areas, just outside the perimeter (picture 6). On the northeast corner was Ann Margret, our most important bunker system set up to protect our camp. No one seemed to know how that bunker system came to be named after the gorgeous actress. It consisted of rooms built with sandbags, with small observation openings in the walls. Soldiers would sit in or on these bunker rooms during guard duty, looking out over the Ho Bo Woods. Here are two soldiers from my platoon on top of one of the sandbag walls (picture 7). Sitting on top of these bunkers, posing for pictures, was popular. An orderly room clerk in our unit took this picture of me, posing with a weapon on the sandbags (picture 8). During my time there, a large part of those woods was cleared with Agent Orange and the debris bulldozed away to make our base camp safer (picture 9).

One night, a group of soldiers was walking toward the bunker for guard duty. One of them was carrying a claymore mine to set up outside the perimeter, so that he could detonate it remotely if he saw any VC. This was routine. Somehow he hit the detonator button while he was walking and blew himself up. That was that.

Cu Chi Base Camp was like a small city. It was south of the Iron Triangle, with the jungle above us and the delta with rice paddies in the more low-lying area. There was an airport that could accommodate large aircraft, a helipad, an area for weapons silos, the 12th Evacuation Hospital with an area for medical evaluation, and a small golf course. Our base camp housed the 116th, the 184th Assault Helicopter company, the 2nd of the 27th division known as the Wolfhounds, the 5th Mechanized Infantry unit with recon abilities, and our artillery unit, all a part of the 25th. I was assigned to the 4th of the 23rd of the 25th Infantry Division, Company C of the Tomahawks Mechanized Infantry Unit for my one year deployment. This unit was made up of six platoons; there were four fighting platoons; A, B and C were infantry platoons and D was the mortar platoon. There was a mechanic's platoon to repair APCs and equipment in the field, consisting of two mechanics and a driver, in a very large, armored, tank-like vehicle called a track. This vehicle had a boom and carried the parts to assemble small, temporary bridges to cross small rivers. You can see the bridge pieces on top. It also had two hatches like an APC, and a shovel affixed to its front. Here I am, sitting in the driver's hatch of one of these mechanic's track, with one of our pet dogs (picture 10). In this next picture, I am standing on the back of their vehicle, where the boom is located (picture 11). They often had to pull a vehicle out of the mud, realign the treads on an APC, or make other repairs. There was a headquarters platoon with the captain and other officers. Each platoon had four squads, with approximately seven men in each squad, although it was supposed to be ten. Every squad had a designated leader, and one member of the squad always doubled as the radioman. There were not enough men to populate these squads. We lost men all the time.

There was an enlisted men's club where you could relax, drink and play some nickel and dime slots. Here are two of my fellow soldiers, posing next to one of our homemade camp signs (picture 12). The Cougars sign to the right in that picture is for one of the enlisted men's clubs on base. Here I am, next to the same sign, with the same pet dog (picture 13). On the jukebox we usually played music from groups like The Temptations or The Four Tops. The black guys were fascinated by how well some of us white guys from New Jersey could dance. They said they never knew any white guys back home who could dance like them. We had the Armed Forces radio network, and they would start each day by shouting, "Good Morning, Vietnam." Then they would play the Beatles song *Good Morning, Good Morning*. Hearing familiar music was a reminder of life back home. I wrote to my mother and asked her to buy me a record player, and included a list of the 45s I wanted. A few weeks later my package arrived. It was battery operated so I could play it anywhere and we often took it with us in our APC. I bought batteries for it at the PX.

There was also a non-commissioned officer's club which I could go to once I became a Sergeant E-5. This club atmosphere was different, these men were older and most were lifers, in for twenty years or more. It was not as much fun, but better booze, better slots, pigs feet in a big jar of vinegar that tasted like the ham we had in the States, and hard-boiled eggs in big jars of vinegar sitting on the bar. Drinking was a favorite pastime for many of us soldiers, whichever club you could go to. We needed something to distract us from what was going on. The favorite drink in any of the bars on base or in the cities was Whiskey and Coke.

We tried not to miss an opportunity to amuse ourselves while trying to stay alive. Here is a picture of a soldier from another squad who often played his guitar around base camp (picture 14). He is standing next to a Jeep with an assigned driver, which was always ready to transport officers. When I was there we had a pet monkey at base camp. One of the soldiers he was often with was Knox (picture 15). The monkey had belonged to another soldier whose tour had ended, and he left it in the care of everyone and anyone at base camp. It had been taught to sit on shoulders, take cigarettes out of breast pockets and take them to his owner. With his owner gone, he would just take them from one soldier's pocket and give them to another. The monkey was still at base camp when I left, getting scraps of food from soldiers and stealing cigarettes.

An important outlet to relieve stress and anxiety during this time in the jungle was playing cards, I always did well with poker. Having Frank as my buddy had a lot of perks. I won a lot and Frank would hold onto the cash for me. He took care of my money because we played in the jungle, and I sure didn't want to lose any of my winnings while trying to stay alive. Payday was once a month, it did not matter where you were, everyone got paid. Some men chose to have the army hold onto some of it or send it to someone back home. Frank would come out by chopper and pay everyone in military payment certificates. That is when the gambling would start, most of us played poker. We all got our regular pay, mine was $180 a month and I got an additional $80 a month combat pay. The largest denomination was $10. That was how I went on all of my R&Rs and had plenty of money to spend. When Frank got out of the Army he went to college and became a CPA. You could trust him with your money and your life.

There was a commissary and a PX at Cu Chi Base Camp. The commissary sold food and the PX sold a variety of items. After I was paid for the first time, I went to the PX and bought a Seiko watch and a Minolta camera. You can see in my pictures that I was always wearing that watch. All the Vietnam pictures in this book were taken with that camera. After my first assignment into the jungle, which lasted several days, I went back to the PX and bought a cooler for our APC.

Every few months a rep from an American car company would be there. You could order a car, and have it delivered through a local dealership back in the States. Payment was not required until the car was picked up. When I was a little more than halfway through my tour, I ordered a 1968 Pontiac GTO at the PX. With Frank's help, I had been regularly sending some of my pay and my poker winnings home to my mother. The car was delivered to my home in Teaneck by a local Pontiac dealer. My mother paid him with that money and took care of all the paperwork. It was a great feeling to know that my new car was waiting for me.

There were the Doughnut Dollies. This group of civilian women, volunteers under the Army Special Services Program, came into existence in the Korean War. At that time, they were known for serving doughnuts and coffee to servicemen, as well as just spending time with them, doing as much as possible to boost morale. In Vietnam, still known as Doughnut Dollies, these volunteers again did so much for young men far from home. In my war, they rarely gave out doughnuts. Instead, they had other items and snacks from home to give us. They wore crisp, light blue dresses like uniforms and looked as much like the girls back home as possible. Many had the familiar American girl ponytail. After signing up and receiving two weeks training, they were shipped out for a year of service. They coordinated with the Red Cross and the USO to bring entertainment and companionship to the troops. They were at our recreation centers and clubs on base, and were always visiting the men at our hospital. Many letters sent home were in their handwriting because many of our wounded could not write. They occupied hooches in base camp, ate Army food, and traveled around by military vehicle and chopper, just like we did. They played cards with us, danced with us and sat talking with us for hours. We appreciated their company very much and we always treated them with respect.

Bob Hope brought one of his famous shows to Cu Chi while I was there, everyone was invited. My squad was able to be in base camp at the time and it was an amazing show. Ann

Margret was with him and I will never forget watching her sing and dance on that stage. Other stars and celebrities were there, too. Thousands of guys were sitting on the ground, on benches, standing on Jeeps and on everything else. They had climbed onto roofs and up utility poles to watch. For those few hours, we did not think about the war.

An amazing fact was that our base camp was built above a large tunnel complex where the Viet Cong lived, slept, and ate, called the Tunnels of Cu Chi. When the 25th Division came from Hawaii by ship in 1965 to build our camp, they had no idea that they were building on top of one of the largest tunnel systems in South Vietnam. Our area was secure, except at night, when the Vietcong would pop up and attack with satchel bombs and small arms fire. The VC, or Charlie as we called them, would wreak havoc, then slip back down into the tunnels and disappear. As time went on we realized just how sophisticated and extensive the tunnel system was. It was developed when the Vietnamese people were fighting the French in the 40s and 50s, then expanded. It was a maze with underground mess halls, munitions storage, hospitals and places to sleep. They ate dry fish and whatever they could kill or scavenge. The tunnels had ventilation systems so that they could stay down there a long time. I have even seen groups entertaining the VC on little stages in the tunnel system. The entrances to these tunnels were very well disguised and booby-trapped. There were many entrances and exits, and fake entrances and exits that led to traps if you were unskilled, unaware or just unlucky. They had trap doors that led nowhere and trap doors that collapsed when you walked on them, causing you to fall into a pit with carefully arranged punji sticks. The punji sticks were sharp and faced upwards, and always had something on them like poison or human feces to cause severe infections or gangrene.

When it was necessary for someone to go into the tunnels, our platoon leaders would ask for volunteers. It was never an order. Large or tall men could not safely maneuver down there. I was short and slim and went in a number of times. Those of us who did this were called tunnel rats. It was extremely dangerous but had to be done, and I was good at it. Before going into a tunnel, I would usually drop a grenade into the opening to eliminate any threats. Not many things were scarier than crawling through those tunnels with a dim light on your head. A bright light would make you an easy target. I carried a 22 pistol with a silencer so as to not blow out my ear drums. After a while we began to use machines that pumped green smoke into the holes to see where the legitimate openings were. Sandy Loudis, another tunnel rat, is someone I did not know over there, but became friends with years later. We often met up at reunions, kept in touch, and he helped us a lot with this book. Cu Chi Base Camp had the tunnel complex under it when I arrived and it still had the tunnel complex under it when I was sent home.

One day, my unit commander came to me and asked me to speak to a newspaper journalist from the Newark Evening News. The reporter's name was Vincent deP. Slavin and he was doing a story about the Tunnels of Cu Chi. My unit was temporarily in base camp after having been out in the jungle for about 30 days on search and destroy and ambushes. We were enjoying a few days to shower, get into clean clothes, rest, eat some hot food and get ready for the next operation. I said yes and the next day he was in our base camp for the interviews. He asked a lot of questions, and I talked about the tunnels and what it was like to go into them. His article was published on August 11, 1967. My mother wrote to me to tell me that she had read the article, and would cut it out and save it for me to read when I got home. I remember thinking at the time *right, if I ever get home.* The article was great, when I finally got home and was able to read it. He wrote about everything we talked about (Appendix I). A few years later, he contacted my parents to find out if I made it home and how to get in touch with me. My mother gave him my phone number and we set a time for a phone interview. He wanted to do another article about what my life was like after Vietnam. By this time, he was working for The Bergen Record and did another great interview with me. He promised to let me know when the article would appear. I did not hear back from him, and found out through the newspaper that he had passed away. They wanted to print his last article about me but never received it. I had to let it go at that.

Since I was the company armorer, it was my responsibility to repair weapons during and after combat, issue weapons to the men and keep a record of the serial numbers. I could disassemble weapons and put them back together blindfolded. That was part of the training I had received at Quartermaster School in Virginia. Being that I was the company armorer, I could issue myself weapons. That's how I acquired a 22 pistol with a silencer, an M60 machine gun, an M14-E2 automatic rifle with a bipod (a small, two-legged base), a 5 round pump shotgun, an M79 grenade launcher, a 45 caliber pistol and an M16 automatic assault weapon. I assigned a variety of weapons to everyone in the 4th of the 23rd.

At first we were still being issued M14 automatic rifles, which were excellent and had been in use since the Korean War. They would fire under water or after being immersed in water, never jammed after getting wet, but were heavy and cumbersome. About a month after I arrived they were replaced with the M16, a much lighter weapon but with a tendency to jam. The M16 fired a small round like a 22 bullet which would move around at a high velocity while traveling through the air, and would still be moving around when it entered the body. One of these could enter the target's leg and come out his back. This weapon was devasting and was something we relied on, but the jamming problem needed to be corrected. The original bolts in these M16s were aluminum, and thinking that this was the problem, the Army engineers sent us steel bolts, and had us replace them all. The jamming persisted until we solved the problem ourselves. We had been using oil on the bolts, but the solution was just the opposite. We experimented and realized that the oil was attracting dirt and sand, and that the solution was to keep the bolts clean and dry. So, wanting to stay alive, we were always removing those bolts, cleaning them and keeping them dry.

I preferred to carry the M60 machine gun and would wrap the bandolier of ammunition around my chest criss-cross. The

M60 is still in use today and is an excellent piece of machinery. In close proximity firefights, it was reliable and would mow the enemy down. Another weapon we had was the howitzer, a family of small cannons. The 90 millimeter ones could be affixed to vehicles or wheelbases. The 105s were permanently affixed to a wheelbase and were pulled by vehicles, usually Jeeps. The largest 155s and 175s were permanently attached to vehicles resembling tanks, with the driver's seat at the rear left. We usually kept all of our hand-held weapons locked in our APC unless they were needed. When we were patrolling or outside our APCs we carried one or more of them. Losing your weapon in a non-combat situation was a court-martial offense.

In the early years, the Vietcong had World War I and World War II weapons, acquired from the French in the 40s. But soon after that they were armed with AK47s, gas operated assault rifles, developed and supplied by the Soviet Union. The 47 stands for the year 1947 when the design was completed. As the war dragged on, Russia and China supplied much of the weaponry used against US forces and the South Vietnamese Army.

About 40 miles north of our base camp was the city of Tay Ninh. This was the Black Virgin Mountain area, heavily populated with VC. We were often there for search and destroy, and American forces would be engaging the Vietcong there for many years. While in that area we would often travel through small villages of enterprising civilians. When they heard that American soldiers would be passing through, they opened up for business. These roadside markets were a welcome distraction for young soldiers. They would sell eggs with chicken embryos in them, a Vietnamese delicacy, that were eaten raw. There were tiny ice cream cones for two cents. They would trap exotic animals in the jungle and sell them to the servicemen. One time, at one of the markets in Tay Ninh, I bought an aardvark and named him Arty. I kept him as a pet for a few weeks and then let him go back into the jungle. There would be barber shops set up for us. Gambling would be set up outside and they played a local game with dice similar to craps. Most of us had some local money in our pockets called piastre, which is what the locals preferred, but they also accepted our military payment certificates. They were very poor and sold anything they could, and there were always young women in these villages selling sex. They were very pretty and sweet to us and often had young children or elderly parents to provide for. In this setting, it usually meant going with them to have quick sex in an abandoned shack, on the ground or in a stable. In these villages, we saw mostly women, children, old men and not a lot of men between twelve and forty. The young men were either dead, in the South Vietnamese Army, or they were Vietcong.

There were other villages, a few of them not too far from our base camp, and one of them was of course, Cu Chi. These villages usually had one main dirt road with a few shabby storefronts, bars and of course houses of prostitution. The residents lived in huts. From our base camp, we could easily travel by Jeep to one of these towns for haircuts, to have laundry done, buy things or visit a woman. We could also travel to Saigon, which was about 35 miles from our base camp. Saigon was a more established city and the trip was dangerous. There were groups of young Vietnamese men, mostly con men and thieves, who would prey on American servicemen. They called themselves cowboys. They were desperate and would be on the roads or lurking around the roadside markets or towns. Anything could happen while we were away from base camp so we were always armed and ready. The exception was that sometimes an entire unit had a town secured, which meant that there should not be enemy soldiers there to shoot at us. If that was the case, we would be advised and could walk around relaxed without having to be ready to return fire. We would still be armed.

Frank and I would often travel to Cu Chi together to have our laundry done. Usually, this area was secure. If not, we would be told to be prepared with our M16s. In either case, there were always American MPs (military police) in Cu Chi. On this particular day the town was secure, and we were at the laundry dropping off clothes. A couple of blocks down was a gas station with a two story building on the property. We knew that area well, the second story always seemed to be dark and unoccupied, just used for storage, and had two double swinging doors. That day, the doors swung open and two VC stepped out and opened up with machine guns, killing and wounding civilians and American soldiers. Frank and I were inside the laundry building and did not have our M16s, just our 45 caliber pistols, which have poor accuracy for distance firing. It didn't take long for our MPs to take control of the situation and kill both men. Frank and I were safe, but for a few minutes, rounds were flying everywhere. It is probable that they gained access to the building using underground tunnels. It was another day with luck on my side and we went back to base camp unharmed.

One of my best friends over there was Herbert Sherrill from the town of St. Albans in New York. He was a big 6' 2" black guy who was just an outstanding man and he called me his little buddy. I am 5' 4". He was too big to ever go into a tunnel. Here he is, with two other soldiers from our base camp (picture 16). We were in different platoons, but the same Unit, 4th of the 23rd Company C. He was a sergeant E-6 and we often walked together in the jungle, sometimes back to back. He was a great person, smart and savvy, and he was always there for me. He went to Hawaii on R&R to spend time with his wife and she surprised him with the news that she was divorcing him. I do not know any more about what happened between them and he did not volunteer anything. He was different after that and began to disregard the rules you need to stay focused and alive during a firefight and it got him killed (Appendix II). I was in base camp when he died in the Binh Duong Province in June 1967. He was one of my best friends over there and it is so sad that my friendship with him was over too soon. He would say he couldn't believe that I had more soul than a lot of his black brothers. I still talk to him today in Heaven, he was that important to me. Here he is again, standing with Knox (picture 17).

Another very important, lifelong friend from Vietnam is Bill Dillehay, one of the soldiers in my squad who went on a lot of overnight ambushes and search and destroy missions with me. Bill was from Texas and joined our unit a short while after my arrival. We would often talk about our plans after we got home. I kept in touch with him and would see him at some of our reunions. Bill has been struggling for years with multiple health problems resulting from exposure to Agent Orange. As of May 2024, he is still alive. There is more about him in the last chapter.

Vinny from New Jersey was another friend who arrived around the same time as I did, but did not report to Hackensack with me. He was promoted to Sergeant E-6 and leader of 2nd Squad when his squad leader was killed, just like me (picture 18). He had excellent instincts and we were often together in firefights and on the trails. Vinny and I remained friends, spoke often and saw each other for years after we returned home. He cannot speak to me anymore, PTSD has affected him, and I remind him of things he does not want to remember. One day while Kathy and I were visiting his home, while his wife and kids were there, I had a PTSD episode. I was not able to sit still, could not relax and felt dizzy. He could not get over seeing a fellow Vietnam Veteran have an attack like that. It was after this visit that he stopped talking to me, would not take my calls, or call me back. That was sad for me. As of May 2024 he is still alive. I know this because some other men in my unit are still in touch with him. They tell me he has been suffering from PTSD for years and is now 100% disabled by it.

Eddie Lowenstein, the one I temporarily roomed with when I first arrived, was from Bakersfield, CA. He was a hoot. He did three tours, and his favorite saying was, "Let's stop and smoke the situation over" anytime we were in a dangerous place. We always had pot and beer. He would have an M16 in one hand and a beer or a joint in the other. He was as close to a hippie as you could be in the jungles of Vietnam. He was in 2nd platoon, 1st squad, so we were almost always together in the field. Years later, one of my favorite things was sitting on my back porch, with a glass of wine and a cigar, talking to him on the phone several times a week. We lost Eddie in 2018 from Agent Orange problems and emphysema from smoking. It was another sad day for me.

My friend Bradley was a Sergeant E-5 with the 5th Mechanized unit, a recon company. They would go out ahead of the fighting units, looking for signs of the enemy. We called him Bad Brad. It didn't matter where we were in the jungle, or what we were doing, Brad would always be impeccably groomed, always have perfectly pressed fatigues and his boots were always shined and clean. I do not know how he did it. We had radios in our APCs with around 240 channels, so he and I would pick a frequency to talk on late at night. Brad called himself a Valley Boy. He claimed to have known Charles Manson and said that he had tripped on acid with him. His APC had a big yellow banana painted on the side and he called it Mellow Yellow. Yes, he was a fan of Donovan, the folk singer from Scotland. One day his APC drove over a mine and the vehicle was damaged, but Bad Brad and his squad walked away. Here he is, standing next to his damaged APC (picture 19). Then I stood next to it, and he took this picture of me (picture 20). I do not know if he is still alive or how he is, we neglected to exchange contact information and I never knew his last name.

One of the first soldiers I became friendly with was a door gunner on a Huey gunship. He had already begun suffering the effects of having to shoot and kill people, and was using drugs trying to cope with the job he had to do. He would administer serious drugs intravenously, causing a recurring abscess in his arm, making it sometimes impossible for him to do his job. Other times he realized that he was in such a drug-induced haze that lives would be in danger if he manned his post. Every chopper took off with a pilot and co-pilot, in case one of them got wounded or killed. While these choppers were engaged their doors were always open, with a gunner manning a 60 caliber mounted machine gun on each side. A few times, if I was in base camp and available, and if his problems were worse than usual, I would take his place on the chopper. This was relatively early in my tour before our squad was going out all the time. The pilots allowed this as long as I did the job. Well, this particular day we were transporting three VC prisoners from where they were captured, to be turned over to the South Vietnamese Army in Saigon. Our US forces never kept VC prisoners. Accompanying the prisoners were South Vietnamese soldiers, we were just an escort. All of a sudden I heard a commotion as one of the South Vietnamese Soldiers started screaming at the prisoners. Although I did not understand the language, it sounded like a violent interrogation. Then he threw one of them out of the chopper and started yelling at the next one, then threw him out. It happened so fast. We were flying at about 1,500 feet so this was just plain murder. Their hands were tied behind their backs. When he started on the last one I grabbed and restrained him and stopped him from killing the last VC. We landed and the ARVN soldiers on the ground took custody of the remaining prisoner.

One of the things we began to realize is that the US was not trying to win that war. I am not sure what their objective was but it was not to win. This put us ground soldiers in danger. We had no-fire zones. Whoever heard of a no-fire zone in jungle warfare? There were times when we were being hit with small arms and mortars and our orders were to not fire back. Certain tactical method rules had to be applied inside a no-fire zone. This was ridiculous nonsense. Our fighter pilots were always in danger of being shot down by sams (surface to air missiles). Then, if they had to parachute out and were captured, they were humiliated, tortured and imprisoned. At the same time, when it was learned that a pilot had dropped bombs into a no-fire zone, where these sams were, he was disciplined and sometimes put on trial for disobeying orders. If we were there to save the South Vietnamese people from communism we could have been sent to defeat the North. As it was, we had been sent to kill these people in their own country. We saw that a lot of targets in the North that had been bombed had no real importance. It seemed to me we were wasting a lot of ammo, rockets, bombs, artillery rounds, and that some people with munitions factories in the US were making a lot of money at the expense of young men's lives. It is said that we dropped more bombs in North Vietnam than we did in all of World War II. Imagine being out in the field, fighting a war like this in a foreign country. Sniper fire, mortars, bombs, napalm, booby traps and mines were just a part of everyday life for us. In base camp or out in the field, the sound of B52s flying around often kept us awake all night. If you were sleeping when a 2000 pound bomb hit, you were bounced into the air.

Church service was held on Sundays, even when we were out in the field, and I became an altar boy. Our priest had been in the army for a while and was now a major, clergymen come in at the rank of captain. Unless it was impossible to land because of fighting, he traveled out by chopper to one of our units every week. He was a great, down to earth man, but also a real man of the cloth. He carried a special M16 assault rifle with a pull out handle that transformed it into a full sized weapon. To me he was very cool. He listened to our feelings about being there and we talked to him about anything and everything and what we had to do to survive. Church was important to us and we prayed for ourselves a lot, I know I always did. The Mass was Catholic, but soldiers of different denominations attended anyway. One Sunday during church we started taking enemy fire, then mortar rounds started coming in. We hit the ground and began firing back. I looked next to me and there was the priest firing at the enemy alongside us. He was a hell of a guy with no fear.

Well, one day after Mass I was talking to our priest and I said to him, "How is it that you carry a weapon and shoot at the enemy? You're a priest." He said, "God sent me here to help you boys. You are young and you are already in hell. I came here to help, not die, so I will protect myself at all times. I am here to save your souls and your lives. After being in hell for a year you have to go home and somehow get back to a normal life." Well that was easier said than done. Every day was a challenge. Everything we did stayed with us.

SEARCH AND DESTROY

When I arrived in January 1967, it was the start of Operation Cedar Falls. This took place deep inside the Iron Triangle, one of the most dangerous places in South Vietnam at the time. Officially this maneuver lasted about three weeks. It was said that an officer's lifespan in the Triangle could be minutes. It was my first day out, and we were in our APCs riding through the jungle. My vehicle was in the front, and I saw my first Vietcong. He popped out of a hole and started firing at us. I grabbed my M14, aimed at the hole, and when he popped up again I fired and blew his head off.

We moved through the jungle in our very noisy vehicles, single file, riding over trees, plants and debris in front of us, which made even more noise. Here is a picture of another squad from my platoon, getting ready to move (picture 21). Being in an APC (armored personnel carrier, the model we used was the M113A) was somewhat safe, but it often meant that the enemy knew where we were. Each squad was assigned its own APC.

RPGs (rocket-propelled grenades) could penetrate the sides, but small arms fire could not. My vehicle was always point, the lead vehicle, and depending on the situation, we could ride inside, walk alongside, or sit on top. There are two hatches in an APC. In the front, left corner was the driver's hatch, where he could have his head sticking out while driving, or close that hatch and sit lower to look through a small window. The TC hatch is the other one, positioned front and center, with a 50 caliber machine gun mounted in front of the opening. It was always loaded and ready to fire with a belt of 50 caliber rounds coming out of an ammo box, with every fifth a tracer round. The soldier in that weapon's seat had a special helmet with a microphone to communicate with the driver, captain or other officers. He flipped a switch to control whom he needed to talk to. One day, early in my tour, we hit a mine while I was riding in the TC hatch. I went flying through the air and landed on the dirt road. I was lucky to only be bruised. After that, whenever possible, I walked alongside. When it was too dangerous to walk alongside, I would take that station in the open TC hatch again.

Every squad leader had a special helmet with a built-in radio, which allowed him to communicate with the driver, XO (executive officer) and captain. The captain, a part of the headquarters squad, would be in constant communication with MACV (Military Assistance Command Vietnam), the brain trust (yeah, right) of the Army. The XO of our platoon would be in communication with all the squad leaders and gave the orders. He was an important target, so his location in the platoon changed frequently while we were moving.

Sometimes, when we were out in the jungle overnight, I would dig a hole to sleep in. Shovels were carried in a pouch on our backpacks. The handle folded in across the blade, making it compact and easy to carry, quick to unfold when needed. By sleeping below ground level, I could avoid being hit by shrapnel from mortar rounds if we were near fighting. In the hole, the round would have to make a direct hit to seriously wound or kill me. One evening, when we were setting up for another night in the jungle, the men in my squad began having a very active discussion about who was going to sleep where. I was not a part of that, having already decided that I would sleep in a hole that night. The back hatch door was open so that we could walk in and out of the APC and I had just stepped outside with my shovel to start digging my hole. We were not expecting any action that night, so we were playing music, and *Tell It Like It Is* by Aaron Neville was on my record player. As I stepped off the metal an RPG hit our APC and the blast threw me a few feet. When I went back to check, all four men inside were killed, two were decapitated. That was an awful thing to see. A few years later, at my parent's home in Bayville, NJ, that Aaron Neville song came on the radio. My mother said out loud, "I hate that song." She never said things like that. I had never told her that story.

After a night of being out on ambush, we would completely break down our temporary base camp and be mobile during the day for search and destroy. One evening, while we were still traveling toward our temporary campsite to set up for the night, we received information that the enemy was close by. Our mortar platoon was alerted and began firing at the designated coordinates from one of their APCs. A mortar platoon APC was just like ours, but with a permanently affixed, rotating weapon capable of firing devastating 81mm mortars. The sound of that, if you were on that APC, would go through you. It was dusk, and I snapped this picture of the men holding their hands over their ears (picture 22). We continued to our temporary campsite and were safe that night.

February 1967 marked the start of Operation Junction City, a three month offensive that kept us in firefights almost every day. We were told that the primary goal of this mission was to locate the VC headquarters, but for much of that time the enemy had been using locations in Cambodia for this purpose. We stayed in our APCs as much as possible for protection, while doing quick trips into Cambodia to strike and get back over the border. Officially, we were not supposed to attack them there, because our leaders feared that attacking them in Cambodia would escalate the war. Unofficially, our commanders ordered these raids. The VC freely used that country as a staging area to regroup, obtain supplies and come back at us. Often, the Vietcong would do heavy damage to the Cambodian village they were occupying, and then find ways to blame the US troops. This drove many civilians to the side of the Vietcong, making it even harder for us to stay alive. We inflicted heavy losses on the VC in Cambodia during this time, but we took heavy losses also.

We had many encounters with the enemy in this Black Virgin Mountain area where they could quickly retreat back over the border into Cambodia. We needed to finish these battles so that they could not come right back and attack us again. Imagine being forced into another country, that was officially off-limits, to engage the enemy. The Ho Chi Minh Trail came from the north through Cambodia and then back into Vietnam. The Vietcong that were hiding there at this time knew we had fighting platoons in temporary, overnight base camps in this mountainous area just outside of Tay Ninh. On this particular night, they decided to attack with mortars and RPGs and retreat over the border again. We followed and stayed hidden in Cambodia overnight, hoping to catch them in the morning. These were quick decisions, and it was a bad place to be unless you had a lot more men than a squad or even a platoon, which we didn't. We were usually outnumbered in this area. We could not locate them and retreated back over the border to the safety of our temporary base camp at Tay Ninh. A few weeks after this encounter, a group came over the border again and conducted another early morning attack with mortars, RPGs, and this time also with heavy artillery. We sustained two casualties and some wounded at our temporary base camp. We fired our mortars and chased them back over the border again and continued pushing them back. I don't know how many we killed, but the attacks stopped for a short while. That day, I wanted to call in an air strike on the enemy in Cambodia but I knew that headquarters would not follow through with it. The US carried out some aerial strategic bomb strikes in Cambodia, but we were not supposed to be going over the border like that.

Cambodia had nothing to do with the Vietnam War except that the VC used it to move men, supplies and weapons.

Following that was Operation Manhattan, conducted in the Iron Triangle along the banks of the Saigon River. We were set up for this in the area of the Ho Bo Woods, right outside of Cu Chi, which included the Boi Loi Woods. Jungle clearing teams would be operating in the field with us a lot during this time. We found and disrupted a number of enemy camps and destroyed any supplies they had. It was search and destroy as much as possible, which was what we were doing every day anyway, and trying to stay alive.

On one of my first excursions into the jungle I met Dennis Reilly, who became a lifelong friend. He was one of the forward observers who worked with all four fighting platoons in our infantry company. The importance of this position cannot be overstated, and was reflected in how the VC rated their kill priority; XO first, forward observer second. We did not always have a forward observer in the field with us. Somewhere in headquarters, the officers decided if and when one of these scouts would be assigned to which units and for how long. He would maneuver around ahead of us, and using a compass, a paper map and his wits, would radio back to us what he observed and what routes were safe. Sometimes a dog and handler would be sent out by chopper to work with him, and a few times it was decided that the area we were in was so dangerous that our unit would be assigned two dog teams. He would coordinate with both of them at the same time. These decisions were made by captains and XOs.

The dogs we worked with were amazing, German Shepherds or Black Labs, and they could smell the Vietcong from a mile away. They were chosen and trained at Lackland Air Force Base in Texas and knew American smells from Vietnamese smells. Both breeds could detect booby traps, the ingredients in bombs, all types of explosives and any disturbance in the jungle undergrowth. We would go out on patrol at different times and the dogs had different jobs. The German Shepherds could smell Vietcong breath and were used when we were on boats or near rivers. Enemy combatants used hollow reeds to breathe through while swimming quietly under water to attach explosive devices to the bottoms of our boats. Our dogs could smell their breath coming up through the reeds and alert their handlers. Both breeds could smell the enemy anywhere near the paths, hear sounds that we could not, and sniff out snipers in trees. The Labs were used a lot for tracking. They were especially helpful in locating the openings to tunnels. Sometimes a chopper would come to bring the dog team back to Cu Chi after a day of working, and sometimes the dog and handler would stay with us overnight. They would wake up to any dangerous sounds or smells. All the dogs were taught to never bark and just silently alert the handler. These dog teams were invaluable and the information they provided saved the lives, and a lot of limbs, of many American soldiers.

The dogs that I saw were not trained to attack anyone, nor did I ever see anyone try to use them in that way. Trained only to smell, listen and alert the handler, they were not a danger to anyone. Most of them did not come home. When the

United States pulled out the troops, the Department of Defense classified the dogs as equipment. They were either handed over to the Army of South Vietnam, euthanized, or just abandoned there. Of the 5,000 dogs that went to Vietnam, only about 200 made it home to retire. In 2000, Robby's Law was passed by Congress and signed by President Clinton. It is H.R.5314, "To require the immediate termination of the Department of Defense practice of euthanizing military working dogs at the end of their useful working life and to facilitate the adoption of retired military working dogs by law enforcement agencies, former handlers of these dogs, and other persons capable of caring for these dogs." At reunions and gatherings, I have seen men cry over the memory of having to leave a dog behind.

Dennis Reilly and a dog team were out in the jungle with us one day in the Iron Triangle area. We were running point, as usual, and an enemy combatant began firing at us. He would pop up and fire and then disappear. We couldn't pinpoint the sniper position, so Dennis and the dog team went in. That dog knew what was expected of him and pointed to the exact tunnel where the sniper was firing from. We hid and waited for him to pop up again. When he did I tossed a seven second grenade into the hole. Boom, sniper dead.

Deep in the jungle was triple canopy, meaning that only streaks of sunlight came through the foliage. It was surreal. Vietnam had a very wet monsoon season and a not so wet drier season, wet from April to September and then not as wet from October to March. The wettest are July and August and the driest are December and January. During the rainy season it rains pretty much every day, this means you are wet all the time, and it is always very hot and humid. Often, when we had to jump into elephant grass from a helicopter, we got pinned down, and it was hours stuck in the mud before we were able to safely come out. But in the Delta it is different, from May to December it is raining, and the drier season is from November to April. Vietnam is below sea level so your feet are always wet no matter what season it is. It means your feet rot. We had rare dry spells too, which meant we could be hit with surprise sandstorms. We could be temporarily blinded while out in the field. Once we had a sandstorm hit us at base camp (picture 23). It looks like snow in my picture.

The Vietcong wore pants like pajama bottoms that could be rolled up to look like shorts, usually without a shirt or shoes, and of course the conical straw hat. It was the clothing of a peasant, same clothing as those working the fields and rice paddies, making it impossible for us to know farmer from combatant. In many cases they were both, farmer during the day, combatant at night. In the jungle and the primitive villages, they had no sewer, toilets, running water or electric. To pee or defecate, they would just lift up one leg of their pajama-looking pants and go, not cleaning themselves, not covering it up. We would always dig a hole, cover it up and wipe ourselves.

When it rained it was time to do whatever you needed to do with water. The Vietnamese people would wash in rivers or when it rained, so we often did the same when we were away from our base camp. There were bomb craters everywhere from the 500 to 2,000 pound bombs dropped by our B52s. These craters would immediately fill up with water because of the sea level. They were like swimming pools, so we would wash and swim in them. I just took this in stride with everything else that I witnessed and experienced there. There was always the threat of poisonous snakes, but it was so hot we would just take that chance to cool off for a few minutes. Leeches were in every body of water and would attach themselves to whatever body part they landed on. Holding a lit cigarette up against them was the only way to make them pop out. If you tried to pull them off they would break, leaving the head, causing a lot of bleeding and possible infection.

Sometimes we had other options out in the field, especially welcome if we had been crawling through mud, filth and dung. The Army would send out small tanker trucks with non-potable water, equipped with those same hanging shower bags. Most of us had a clean change of clothes with us in our APCs, and it was a relief to feel clean and dry for a while. Other times, if no combat was expected for a day or two, you could request a chopper back to base camp just to get clean and change clothes. Snipers were shooting at us all the while. Heat and rain, running into the enemy, getting into firefights, mortar rounds coming in all around you, never-ending, day after day. We used to say that if you served in Vietnam, St. Peter lets you right into Heaven because you have already been in hell.

There were spiders with bodies as big as chipmunks and countless varieties of poisonous snakes. We carried special counter-venom snake bite kits that you could pull off your belt and inject into your thigh. There were two-step vipers, king cobras, small apes, red killer ants and of course the dreaded mosquitoes. The mosquitoes carried malaria, encephalitis and dengue fever. The two-step viper was so named because after you were bit, in the time it took you to walk two steps, you were dead. The centipedes and scorpions could be two feet long, and both could bite with a venom that would cause a lot of pain and swelling but usually not kill you. There were tigers and panthers in the jungle. One night on guard duty, I found myself staring at a pair of large, wide-set eyes. I knew exactly what it was. I would never have shot a big, beautiful cat for no reason, and there was no reason to. They wanted nothing to do with us.

We were out on foot patrol one day walking quietly through the jungle when I walked right into a gigantic spider web. It was about six feet wide, and the body of the spider was about six inches in diameter with legs about a foot long. I pulled out my 45 pistol and shot it. Another time we were forced to quickly take cover in one of the APCs, and then realized that a very large brownish/blue spider was inside with us. It jumped on me and bit my hand before I was able to open the back hatch and throw it out. My hand swelled up like a balloon and hurt like hell but I did not get sick. I later learned that it was a tarantula, not usually deadly to humans.

One very hot day in the jungle on search and destroy we got pinned down by automatic fire and one of my men had the misfortune to be under a tree that was loaded with red ants. As weapons fire hit the tree, the ants began dropping on him. He had to stay down or he would have been killed. By the time the VC fled the area he had been bitten thousands of times. I called in a chopper to evacuate him, and by that time his head had swollen to twice its size. Later we learned that he died in the hospital.

One day my squad was ordered to go on ahead to recon before the whole company moved. As soon as we put some distance between us and our platoon, we began taking enemy fire. We were in the rice paddies, which usually had small walls of dirt built up, so we ducked down and used them for cover. I immediately called back requesting mortar fire and gave the enemy's location. I put my hand on top of one of the dirt walls and was stung twice by scorpions. We were still under fire so we could not move away from the nest. My hand hurt and swelled up but again I did not get sick or develop a fever. I was lucky it was not one of the more venomous types. The mortars did their job that day so we were able to get out of there and back to our unit safely.

I had a great deal of respect for the Vietcong and North Vietnamese fighters, they were brave and vigilant, fierce soldiers and a force to be reckoned with. I did not have anything against these people, I just wanted to stay alive. One of the things that made this real was that we were in their backyard, so they were familiar with everything. They knew where their booby traps and punji pits were. They knew where all the tunnels were and the location of all the escape hatches, it was their ball in their court. This was their country and we were trespassing. Vietnam should have been left alone. Sure, we were in the jungle for months at a time, but this was their permanent home. There was a lot of collateral damage. We would often see burned-out huts in clearings in the jungle (picture 24). Bombs and napalm were occasionally dropped on entire villages. Sometimes women, children or old men tripped their own booby traps and were maimed or killed.

Our mission was to help the Republic of Vietnam not become a communist country. We were to accomplish this by helping the ARVN, the Army of the Republic of Vietnam. The North Vietnamese Army was allied with the Vietcong in the South to fight the ARVN. The ARVN was a regular army with uniforms, weapons, food and clean water. They were not motivated and had nowhere near the commitment or fortitude that the enemy had. I do not see how they could ever have defeated the North Vietnamese Army, even with our help. The Vietcong, on the other hand, were determined to win their country back. Many times, American soldiers needed help against the North and only ARVN units were in the area. They would be called in to help, but after confirming that they were coming, would just not show up, leaving the soldiers of the United States to fight alone. Sometimes, if we suspected that VC were hiding in a village, we would go in forcibly, relocate the civilians, their belongings and animals. Anyone then left in the area would be considered an enemy combatant, and we would burn down what was left of the village. Any men or women that we captured would be turned over to the ARVN as prisoners for interrogation, and we often witnessed them treating VC prisoners horribly. We knew that most of those enemy soldiers would never make it back to their families. We knew that was not right and there was nothing we could do about it. I never saw our Army mistreat or torture enemy combatants. The ARVN soldiers were brutal cowards. The VC almost always defeated them unless we were there to help. I called the ARVN soldiers Pussies, and the VC Badass Mother****ers with no fear. Many of us thought that the Vietcong must have been using drugs because of their fearless behavior. There were always some VC pretending to be ARVNs on the side of the South, and at night they would use the information they had gathered during the day to go out looking for us. Usually, there was an ARVN soldier embedded with our unit while we moved through the jungle. He provided information and guidance, knew the geography, and of course would translate for us when necessary. Most units had an embedded ARVN. We were told that they had been vetted and should be trusted, but we were often suspicious of them.

The VC soldiers were vicious and we all knew what getting captured by them meant. It was better to get shot and killed quickly trying to escape than to be captured and tortured by them. Another thing we had to get used to were the women VC combatants, they were as vicious and brutal as the men. There were stories about women VC soldiers doing things to American prisoners that I cannot write here, which is why the guilt over sometimes having to kill a woman faded quickly. Stories were circulated about devices used by local prostitutes to harm American soldiers, but we often wondered if these were started by our own Army to keep us away from them.

The North Vietnamese soldiers would come down the Ho Chi Minh trail from the north with all their weapons and ammo on their backs. They had trucks, but usually did not use them here because this was dense, canopied jungle and they were hard to maneuver on the trail, which was almost always muddy. We would bomb the trail constantly but they would just come down a different way and change the trail. The trail went through Cambodia too, which we were not supposed to cross into, but many times we did to deal with VC units hiding there.

These search and destroy missions were under the command of General Westmoreland and they failed miserably. He was an experienced military professional, but this war was unlike anything he had ever experienced. There were no front lines like in World War I or II. We would try to set up front lines but the enemy was all around us, and they were always using those cursed tunnels. Most firefights were the result of small units of VC setting up ambushes and striking. Sometimes they just attacked and disappeared before we could react. They knew how to quickly engage us and win these battles despite our superior military strength and equipment. The enemy would bring in supplies and move around at night, their methods and routes changing daily. There was no way we could figure it out or anticipate their movements.

We would be in the jungle sometimes for 30 to 60 days at a time, and most meals in the field were packaged C Rations, left over from the Korean War. Each pack had a protein like chicken, tuna or turkey, and they all tasted the same. Everything was in cans. Beans and franks and fruit cocktail were the best. There were also small packs of cigarettes, 4 in a pack, and gum. Sometimes a helicopter with supplies would land and set up a hot breakfast of powdered eggs, bacon, reconstituted milk and hot coffee. Believe me, when you were soaked from monsoon rains and exhausted from fighting, it was like Heaven dropped in for you. Sometimes at dinner they would fly in hot dogs. If things remained peaceful for a few extra minutes, we could have a cigarette and maybe some pot before moving on. I had smoked cigarettes a little during high school but really became a smoker over there. Men who had never smoked before picked up the habit. It took the edge off our dreadful situation, and they were free. Clean water was sometimes hard to get so we had tablets to drop in the local water if we had to drink it. Of course, diarrhea came later, just dig the hole quickly. One day a wild boar crossed our path, we shot it, dug a pit, fired it with C4 and roasted it. C-4 burns like wood when lit, it needs a blasting cap to explode. Well, it was fucking good and tasted like the best ham we ever had. We would have hunted and barbecued local animals more often if we had not been so busy staying alive.

I grew up in an Italian family. My mother and grandmother made everything from scratch, and everything they made was delicious. Now that I was away from home, my mom would send me a package every two weeks with home-made tomato sauce in a glass jar, spaghetti, dried sausage or pepperoni and Italian bread. Sometimes there would be meatballs or lamb neck bones in the sauce, and sometimes she included wine. First I would boil water in my steel helmet with C-4 and cook the spaghetti. Then, using my mess kit fork I would drain the water, add the sauce from the glass jar and heat it again, all in the middle of the jungle. Blew everybody's minds. Since my good friend Frank was the mail clerk, he would fly out and get my food package to me quickly so everything was relatively fresh. For a short while I would eat like I was back home in Teaneck. Many of us got packages from home with food and other items.

Frank always had helicopter transportation at his disposal and could request a flight out to us anytime. He would sometimes stay with us in the field for the weekend, and then call a chopper to fly him back to base camp. Other times he would just locate us and drop supplies and treats on pallets. He would bring cold beer and ice, and of course our APC was equipped with that cooler I had bought at the PX. Huge blocks of ice were bought from a local supplier and brought into base camp for us. They were made with non-potable water, stored underground, insulated with something like rice. Frank would break up these blocks of ice before bringing it out to the troops, and it still had that rice-like insulation mixed in with it. It was only used to keep the beer cold. We got Ballantine beer, which we were told was donated, but we still had to pay something for it. We also had Vietnam's bottled beer called Ba Muoi Ba. Weed and other drugs were always available.

We all learned some of the history of the area by just talking about it when we had time on our hands. Long before the Vietnamese people evolved in Southeast Asia, the native MountainYards people lived there. They hunted and foraged in the jungle and were primitive and tribal. Later, they helped the French fight the Japanese in Vietnam, and then they helped the French fight the Vietminh, named for Ho Chi Minh, before they became known as the Vietcong. These people had their own language and were friendly to the American soldiers. The

Vietnamese and the MountainYards usually kept away from each other. We tried training them to kill Vietcong and North Vietnamese soldiers, but this time they chose to not be involved. They eventually moved into the central highlands to get away from all the fighting. I personally only ran into them a few times when I was in that area on search and destroy. It was spelled Montagnards, but we called them MountainYards.

In the 40s and 50s, the French used the South Vietnamese people as cheap labor. In fact, they took advantage of the Vietnamese people for many years. We heard that the French would punish workers who did not cooperate. At the Battle of Dien Bien Phu in 1954 the French were finally defeated and were sent packing, but the Michelin company remained. There, in the jungle, in the Binh Duong Province, northwest of Saigon, was Michelin's 31,000 acre rubber tree plantation and mansion. By 1967, all the buildings were run down but the rubber plant was still operating. Here I am, on the plantation, standing next to the rusted girders of one of the abandoned buildings (picture 25). Tires made from natural rubber were a huge business in the 50s and 60s, and this plantation dated back to 1925. The Michelin company paid off the Vietcong to keep the plantation open during the fighting. The work of collecting the rubber, always done by Vietnamese women, continued. The war just went on, there were booby traps, tunnels, Vietcong and American forces fighting and killing each other all over the plantation, while rubber was being collected and processed on this Michelin property. It was another staging and storage area for the Vietcong. The rubber was collected in cups that hung from the trees on hooks or nails. It was later learned that many of the workers would then replace the cups in a certain way to show the VC where we were. That is probably how we got hit all the time while on the plantation. No one suspected anything at the time. Our 25th Infantry spent blocks of time, from May 1967 to December 1967, on the plantation for search and destroy missions. We would ride through in our APCs, knocking down the rubber trees, which the US government ultimately had to pay for. It was said to be $600 a tree, and that was 1967 money. Many years later I learned that rubber trees stop producing rubber at some stage in their lives, and those trees are then cut down and used for furniture. By that time, in my civilian life, I was in the retail furniture business. A headboard fell over in one of my stores one day and I saw the 'Made in Vietnam' label and, wow, did that take me back. The wood from those old rubber trees makes excellent furniture.

In the rice paddies, primarily in the lower lying deltas, it was also business as usual during the war and we sometimes had to cross those areas. We would be open and exposed for miles, vulnerable to mortar and sniper fire. Being careful took on a new meaning here. There would be women, children and old men working the rice paddies, but like everywhere else, they could easily be VC. This particular day we were walking through the paddies and began taking automatic weapons fire. We hit the ground and started slowly crawling through the water. There were 7 of us, just my squad on patrol, and we had to identify the source of the firing and stop it. It was a machine gun nest in the line of the woods. When I got close enough I took a chance, jumped up and threw a grenade, but it blew up too far away to stop them. Then one of my men took the opportunity to get closer and his grenade hit the mark. We killed them, three of them, all young, maybe twelve or thirteen, but we did not know that until we saw the bodies. Heck, we were not much older than them. In the jungle and tall grasses, we usually had no way to know who was firing at us until we saw the bodies. If they were firing at us, we had no choice.

While out on search and destroy in the Boi Loi Woods one day we came across a village. My squad was on point as usual, and most of us were walking instead of riding in or on the APCs. I saw a rifle come out of a window in a hut and the firing started immediately. We hit the ground in a prone position and opened up with our M60 machine guns. When the firing stopped from both sides we saw that the hut had been badly damaged. We went in the front door and it looked like any VC soldiers had fled through a back door, into a tunnel that led to a river. No weapons were found in the hut. We found two women and two children dead inside. We had no way to know that there would be women and children in that situation. That really had an effect on us. When we stepped outside the hut we started getting mortar rounds fired at us and had to retaliate. There was no one left in the village and we were ordered to burn it down and return. To this day that haunts me.

One very rainy morning we started with a search and destroy mission near the Cambodian border, walking slowly and quietly through the jungle. It had been raining all night and the water was flowing down the paths, going into my boots and soaking my feet. We were a platoon-sized force on that day, about 40 men. Dennis Reilly was with us, paired with a dog team. The dog was alerting and pointing straight ahead, which meant either ARVNs or Vietcong, they smelled the same to the dogs. The Vietcong was the enemy, but ARVNs could also turn on us in some situations. It was a large group of Vietcong crossing over from Cambodia to cause havoc with whatever Americans they could find. They turned and started firing mortars at us. We fought back with small arms but were outnumbered. This force was unusually large so I had my radioman call for help. There was a mechanized ARVN unit in the area and they were dispatched to join us but never showed up. We were there to save their country and they were as useless as could be. That day we had a platoon sergeant with us to give orders to the squad leaders, and a 1st lieutenant above him who gave him orders. The decision was made to try to retreat and create some distance between us and the enemy. This was done so that we could call in our 81 millimeter mortars from our artillery unit about two miles back. I radioed the proper coordinates to them, they started firing and were right on target. Our platoon sadly took 2 casualties that day. The rest of us were able to get out of there alive, including Dennis, the dog and handler.

It was a very hot morning somewhere in the Iron Triangle and a dog and handler were with us. We had just finished a C-ration breakfast. It was a beautiful day, the sun was up and a few of my fellow soldiers were standing across an open field by their APC, so I casually took out my camera. Just as I snapped the picture, there was a mortar explosion right behind them (picture 26), and we watched as they hurried into their vehicle. I did not realize when I snapped the picture that I had captured the explosion on film. A few seconds later a second round hit much closer to us. We had not been expecting this kind of activity that day. We headed for the only place we would have any protection which was inside our APC. The hatch door was already down so we were able to get inside quickly and close it. Our dog team went in with us, but we did not realize how hot it would get. The rounds sounded like they were coming in from all around us. I did not find out until later that it was friendly fire. Our own artillery unit was dropping rounds short of their target, and they were landing near us. As the rounds hit and the temperature inside got hotter and hotter, the German Shepherd started foaming at the mouth, and even his handler could not control him. The exploding rounds were now dropping very close by and shaking the APC. There was no way I could open the back hatch door yet and the dog started to come towards us, viciously growling. I had to draw my 45 pistol and shoot him. I hated doing it and still feel bad today, but I had no choice. I did what I had to do. Once the artillery stopped and we were soaked from sweating, I dropped the back hatch. Even though it was probably 95 degrees outside, the fresh air felt cool for a short time. We got out, dug a hole and buried the dog. I had to report to headquarters that I shot it and why. Nothing was ever said about it. No one ever mentioned it again.

We were not usually in our base camp at Cu Chi, but on this particular day we were, when we learned that an artillery unit in the mountainous area of Tay Ninh was getting hit hard and needed help. We loaded up in choppers and jumped out right in the middle of the battle, two squads, fourteen of us. We immediately got down low in the elephant grass trying to stay out of sight, but they knew our location and were advancing so we had to fire back. The artillery unit that had put out the call was equipped with 105 small howitzers, and the Vietcong had overrun their position. This was the first time I had seen an artillery unit overrun like this. The VC had taken control of the howitzers, turned them around, and a number of our men in that artillery unit were already dead or wounded. One of my guys and I got too close and were pinned down immediately by two VC firing at us with AK47s. Then they looked away for a few seconds which gave me an opportunity. I stood up and emptied my M16 into them and connected with every round. One of them jumped on me with his hands on my throat and was dead when we both fell to the ground. We continued firing and eventually the rest of them took off into the jungle and we were able to reacquire the artillery equipment. To take care of the few that were still in the area, one of our commanders called in an air strike. We watched as a Canberra came in low to drop napalm and it never pulled out. A Canberra is a plane with two jet engines on each wing and we called it a Bully English Plane. It could fly at 500 mph and then slow down to 200 mph to drop its load. This time, after it dropped its load and the job was done, it went straight down into the jungle and crashed. Small arms fire probably hit both pilots. We were sent in to see if there were any survivors, there were none, and to retrieve any important equipment. The Vietcong had also seen it go down and were all over it. We had to kill them so we could recover the plane's equipment and the bodies of our brave pilots. We destroyed what was left.

One day we were on search and destroy, moving quietly around some villages we suspected of sheltering the VC. Villagers were often forced to help them, but we could not worry about that or do anything about it. The danger was the same. I had been in country about five months. As we were searching the huts we started taking automatic fire from the surrounding woods. We lost two men in my squad right away and one of them was my squad leader. We returned fire and killed two of them, and the rest disappeared. The next day I was designated temporary squad leader, because I was the one in our squad with the most experience. Within a week orders came down making me a Sergeant E-5 and permanent squad leader of 1st Squad, 1st Platoon of Charlie Company 4th of the 23rd, 25th Infantry Division. I held that position for the remainder of my seven months in country.

There was a lot to learn about how to command and handle a squad. I knew the leader of 2nd squad from our platoon, from base camp and being out in the field together. A few days after my promotion, several squads from our platoon were out in the Boi Loi Woods and began taking small arms fire and he was near me in the firefight. He showed me how to pinpoint the muzzle flash of the enemy weapon and how to instruct my men to open up and spray back and forth over that small area. I learned from him how to silently give hand signals to my men. He taught me a lot about communicating with headquarters at base camp, and with our commanding officers in the field with us. After we were all discharged and back in the States, I did not keep in touch with everyone. Kathy, my wife, is on lists to receive email notifications about men in my platoon and other information about Vietnam Veterans. Around 2017, she received a message posted by his wife, saying that he had passed away from Agent Orange complications. We also learned that he had been struggling with financial difficulties. We, some of the remaining men from our platoon sent some money to his wife to help. It is always sad to hear about a fellow Veteran who did not or could not access the system for assistance. There are ways for Veterans in this situation to get help, but often they are too sick or too depressed to follow through with the paperwork.

Another time my squad of seven men had a small area to search as we headed across rice paddies towards the tree line. We had information about VC activity and we were just on recon to observe and report back. I was used to doing LPs, or being stationed at listening posts, but this was our first long-range recon mission. As we approached the tree line the enemy opened up on us with automatic weapons. We tried to drop behind the small piles of dirt that separated the paddies, but two of my guys got hit before we even had a chance. We fired into the tree line with tracers so that we could see where our rounds were going, trying to aim at their muzzle flashes. Tracers are rounds that leave a tinted trail in the air so that you can see exactly where your bullets are landing. On that day I had made sure that all of the rounds in all of our weapons were tracers. Based on my experience, I had a feeling that we would see this kind of action. I worked up the coordinates of where the enemy was firing from, using a paper map and my eyes. Then I called into a nearby artillery unit requesting hydal bursts to help confirm their location. If the bursts were over the correct location, which I could confirm by sight, I would then ask that artillery unit to fire their heavy artillery at that spot. If I saw that the bursts were not at the right spot, my radio guy would contact them again with a message something like "add 200 meters left" and they would fire another burst. Messages like these might go back and forth a few times until we got it right. Sometimes, the first burst would let them know that we had an artillery unit close by and scare them off. On this day we defined the right spot on the first try, our artillery unit bombarded the area, and the VC firing stopped. That day I never found out if any VC were killed or if they just ran off. I had two wounded men to take care of, so I called in for a medevac chopper for them, and another transport chopper to get us back to Cu Chi to regroup. The next day another chopper took us back out to our unit in the field. When men were wounded or killed, my squad would temporarily be at a loss until replacements were assigned to me, which could happen at base camp or out in the field. That time I was assigned two new squad members at base camp before we were flown out again. It was another day in the rice paddies.

One day my squad was assigned an LRRP (long range reconnaissance patrol) near the border of the jungle down in the delta. On that morning it was rainy, and the heat and humidity were overwhelming. Our job was to locate the enemy and report back so that our unit could plan and execute an attack. We were not supposed to engage the enemy that day. Our small patrol had a very specific job to do and had to be very quiet, because during a maneuver like this, we were at greater risk of being killed or captured. We were often miles away from our unit and protection, and on this day we had traveled about five miles into the jungle surrounding the Iron Triangle. We had to set up the LP and wait for some noise or see movement. There was reliable info that a VC patrol was in the area. The plan was to do our job, quietly move to another location miles away, and radio in our findings. Then we had to find a suitable landing zone, call a chopper to pick us up, hopefully to bring us safely back to our temporary base camp. Unfortunately, things did not go according to plan that day. The VC patrol was a large company of maybe 75 men moving quickly in our direction. They set up base camp for the night maybe 300 meters from where we were. Having no time to run, we had to stay quiet and sit it out. We could not call in mortars, artillery or air strikes of any kind because we were too close. Not only might they hear the crackle of our radio, but we could be blown up ourselves by friendly fire in such a close situation. We could move during the night or just wait till morning to see what they were doing. As squad leader I was responsible for the men I was with, and I knew that being captured by this group would be worse than being killed. Luckily we had C-rations and water with us. None of my men could rest, and a few hours went by. I decided during the night that we had to move. Slowly and quietly we put as much distance between us and them as we could. By morning, we had moved far enough away from them to allow us to use our radio to report the coordinates of that VC group. I called in an artillery strike and waited for a response. The first round came in and it was off by about 100 meters to the left. I had them move the next one over and it came down in the right spot. Then I radioed in to fire for effect, meaning fire to kill. Now that we had the right spot, we got the hell out of there. I called for a chopper to pick us up. We exploded a small, green smoke grenade to pinpoint where it should land, and we boarded and flew back to base camp.

My squad was in the Iron Triangle one day on a search and destroy mission, when we started taking small arms fire. We immediately began firing back with our superior automatic weapons, but they had the advantage again, popping up out of holes and then disappearing back into the tunnels. We went into the jungle at the tree line looking for the tunnels, dropping grenades into whatever holes we found. There were too many of them in this area to chance going into the extensive tunnel system. We just kept dropping grenades into holes and moving in order to be protected from the blowback. I decided to call in an air strike on this area to see if we could do any damage to these tunnels. We just kept backing up until we were clear of danger. Our planes came in and bombed the whole area. We did not see any more movement from those tunnels that day.

I remember one day when we were out in the Boi Loi Woods, two men from our platoon had gone into the tunnels looking for enemy combatants and did not come out. We just knew that something bad had happened and two of us went in after them. They were not far from the opening, both dead from small arms fire. The VC soldiers were gone. I slowly and quietly backed out and called in the Rome plows to dig up the area. We retrieved the bodies of our brave soldiers so that they could be sent home.

The possibility of snipers firing at us or someone stepping on a mine or tripping a wire trap was always there. The enemy could get you without even being where we were. We learned that the traps and poison pits were designed to wound but not kill, to slow down the movement of our troops. This is a very old war technique. It takes valuable time to help a wounded soldier, preventing us from immediately chasing the enemy into the jungle. We would stop and stay with our wounded and make sure they got on the helicopters during a dust-off. A dust-off is when a chopper lands in the jungle to pick up wounded soldiers and then takes off as quickly as possible.

The Black Virgin Mountain area in Tay Ninh, at the edge of the dreaded Iron Triangle, was another home base of operations for the Vietcong. This area was about 3,300 feet above sea level. There were a lot of expertly camouflaged tunnels for them to hide in. Around the tunnel openings you would never see any loose dirt or disturbance, and there were booby traps around the holes. The VC were experts at camouflage. Tunnels would go in different directions, some leading to dead ends so you had to be careful to not get trapped. Somehow I had good instincts and knew which way to go and when to get out.

While patrolling through the jungle one day we reached an area where we had to cross a small river with our APCs. The first one trying to cross got stuck in the mud, so we tried to pull it out with my APC, and next thing I knew both APCs were bogged down. We were sitting ducks, so the remaining vehicles set up to protect the disabled ones. We started taking small arms fire and had to deal with that while I called for help. A Chinook helicopter responded, dropped a hook into the hatch, and lifted and set both APCs back on land one at a time. That was something to see. We finally got everyone across the river at another location and moved on.

I happened to be in base camp another time, filing reports, away from my squad, when a call came in from our unit in the field. They were pinned down and taking on heavy automatic fire, had wounded, needed help and evac choppers. A group of us grabbed our gear, loaded into a chopper and were dropped into the middle of the firefight. No one in their right mind would ever want to land in the middle of that mess, but they needed assistance and the wounded needed to be picked up. One of our crazy warrant officers, that is the designation of a helicopter pilot, takes off from base camp with his co-pilot and radios in to us for smoke to pinpoint our position. We had different color smoke bombs with which to signal the choppers, and we would coordinate with the pilots to know what colors we were using. He was flying in to get the wounded no matter what, circling around looking for the smoke and a place to land, when a VC shoots an RPG at his copter, hits it dead on, and down he goes. A Huey gunship, also a chopper, but not one equipped to transport wounded, who was there to lend air support, sees them go down and picks them up. They fly back to Cu Chi Base Camp and this warrant officer and co-pilot get another medevac chopper and take off. They fly back out, pick up our wounded in the middle of a hell of a firefight and get the two most seriously wounded back to the 12th Evac Hospital in Cu Chi and save their lives. I never learned those hero's names.

Years later, in my civilian life, while working at a furniture store, I became friendly with another salesman named John. We kept in touch. But it wasn't until 2000, when I ran into him in a poker room in a casino, that I learned that his father, we'll call him Ro, was a Vietnam Veteran. Ro was an evac chopper pilot with the rank of captain (above warrant officer), and John told me his story while we played cards. It was late 1967, and our soldiers were in a firefight in the Pleiku Province. There were a lot of wounded and Ro and his co-pilot flew out to pick them up. When they got out to the landing zone, there was hectic fighting everywhere. Small arms fire hit the rocket engine of their chopper, also wounding his co-pilot, and they crashed. So what does he do? He squeezes into the cab of a Huey that is ready to take off, with his wounded co-pilot and other wounded on the sleds, and gets back to base camp. He gets another evac chopper, acquires another co-pilot, and goes back out. He picks up the wounded, drops them off at our 12th Evac, and goes back out again. Nothing was going to stop him from saving lives that day. The fighting was so intense that he got shot down again. What does this hero do? He and his co-pilot get into another Huey for a ride back to base camp, get another chopper and come out again. This time he lands and gets several wounded on board and heads back to base to get these guys to the hospital to save their lives. He was awarded the Silver Star for this. This is what a hero is all about. Those medevac pilots were the heroes of the war. It was all about getting guys to the hospital quickly.

There was another time when we were on search and destroy in the rice paddies again. We were on foot, and our APCs were riding along next to us. Vietnamese women always worked the paddies and the plows were being pulled by water buffalos that weighed about 1,200 pounds. These animals were guided by old men and were not familiar with the smell of American soldiers. One of them broke away from its plow and started to come at us. Both the males and females have big horns, we had seen these animals in action before and knew what they could do. My guy that was closest emptied his M16 into the beast and it did not even slow down. To protect my guy I went into my APC and got my M14, which carries a much larger bullet. Two shots to the buffalo's head and it was dead. I once saw one of these animals step on a mine that would have blown up an APC and it did not die, just lay there screaming. We assumed that both times, the farmer butchered the animals for food. We never stayed long enough to find out.

We were out in the Iron Triangle one day during a search and destroy mission. I was walking with Vinny and we began seeing evidence of tunnels. It was early in my tour so I had an M14, the M16s were not there yet. A head popped up from a tunnel entrance and I saw a woman toss a grenade at Vinny. She did not see me. His back was turned so he did not see her or the grenade. I immediately yelled "Grenade" and shot her in the head. Even so, he would never have been able to move fast enough to avoid the explosion. Lucky for him, the grenade was defective and did not go off. This was a very scary learning experience for both of us, coming so close to this woman VC combatant. I went into the tunnel but found no one else and no supplies, and Vinny and I moved on. It was another day of search and destroy.

We would go through the thick jungle by riding over trees and everything in front of us. My APC was usually in the front, which was both good and bad. It was good because the enemy hit in the middle or back most of the time, bad because if there were mines or booby traps, our vehicle would go over them first. The enemy had trip wires laid out in the jungle and on the paths. They were always tied to a mine, were very low to the ground and almost impossible to see when you are walking. You are thinking about so many things you can't always remember to look for these trip wires. It can kill or take off a foot or leg. The worst part of stepping on one of these wires is when you trip one you usually blow up someone else walking near you. If that happens and someone else is killed or injured, you now have to live with those guilty feelings for the rest of your life. No one could forget something like that. Maybe the best case is that you lose one or both legs and not your life. What we all tried to always do is be careful. Watch where you walk, take your time, and observe your surroundings in all directions. Most of the regular booby traps that are set off by an APC riding over them do not do much harm to anyone inside. If you ride over a 500 pound bomb set to go off when the pressure plate is released, even in an APC, it could mean being wounded or killed.

Some days were really depressing, but we had to remain alert because we were in small scale firefights all the time, involving sniper fire or mortar rounds. We had so many modern weapons against a guy with a rifle in the beginning of 1967. The Vietcong also had mortars that were fired from a reusable, simple hand held tube that they carried on their backs. One soldier would carry the tube and others would carry the mortars. They would just drop the mortar round into the front of the tube and point and fire. We had a similar weapon called a LAW (light anti-tank weapon), it was a cardboard tube in a plastic wrapper. Just remove the wrapper and shoot, it was pre-loaded. For us this type of weapon was disposable, but we always destroyed the tubes before discarding them so that the enemy could not reuse them. It was primarily an anti-tank weapon, but the VC did not have tanks. We would use them to destroy their bunkers. One time, out in the field, I had a defective LAW that had to be destroyed. I put C4 explosive in a hole with a detonator, put the LAW on top of that and pushed the button. I miscalculated, and it shot straight up like a rocket too soon, blew right past my head and singed my hair.

One day, Army Intelligence (an oxymoron) thought up a maneuver for us. They said something like this had been used in World War II. They had our guys go to downtown Cu Chi, hit the bars, act drunk and talk it up about an operation in the Boi Loi Woods. The story was that our company would be set up in a specific location for the night after a search and destroy mission. So we built plywood structures that looked like APCs, painted them, and situated them in a field. Then we brought in plows and dug big holes to hide our real APCs, with our 60 caliber machine guns sticking out. They put the fake wooden structures in front of the real ones. The thinking was that the VC would get close and attack the wooden ones with RPGs, and then we would kill them with the real ones. It did not work. No one attacked. They didn't have formal education but that did not make them stupid.

There were so many officers there doing things that got guys wounded or killed, especially some of the gung-ho ego ridden 2nd lieutenants coming over from the States, after going through office training school. They wanted to be in charge, when they knew nothing about how to fight in the jungle and survive against the crafty and committed Vietcong. Many got killed right away and were replaced with new dummies. The smart ones listened and learned and lived. It really was best for them to pay attention to guys that had been there for months. We knew a lot about the terrain and the enemy. They came over thinking *Hell, I'm an officer. You have to listen to me or be court-martialed.* They arrived and were immediately assigned a platoon, and thought they knew everything. They outranked seasoned soldiers who had real combat experience. Booby traps got a lot of them, they did not understand that jungle warfare is different and that the jungle is unforgiving. I do not know what they taught in those classes. Most of us had the option of going to Officers Training School while still in the States but chose not to, because it meant being in the service for a longer time.

I met one of those new officers after a routine chopper flight brought me back to my unit, somewhere in the Iron Triangle.

This new 2nd lieutenant was assigned to our APC. I realized right away that he was an arrogant jerk. He thought that he knew more than I did. I was a seasoned combat soldier who knew the area and its dangers. We were moving along slowly on Highway One when he stopped our whole column of APCs. Farmers were working their fields harvesting cucumbers. So my 2nd lieutenant thought he would jump off our vehicle and get some cucumbers. I said to him, "Don't touch those cucumbers and don't go near the fields where they are growing." He yelled back at me, "Don't tell me what to do, soldier." There was no way for us to stop him. He walked over to get some cucumbers, hit a trip wire and blew himself to pieces. We had to pick up what was left of him and put the pieces in a body bag. I felt sorry for him, but I was also relieved that no one else was injured. He had been in country for less than a week and was determined to not listen to Grunts. It happened a lot with these officers sent over from the States. We found a location to safely set up for the night.

There was a special incident when we were out on search and destroy with a new captain. I will not name him because as of 2024, he is still alive. He had recently taken over our command when we were assigned to an area that I knew very well. I was point APC, as usual, and he had us headed in the wrong direction. Our lieutenant was also new, and I called back to him. I was in the TC hatch behind the 50 caliber machine gun, talking to him through my radio headgear. I told both of them that we were going in the wrong direction. I had been in country about six months at this time. They paid no attention to what I told them and we circled around to the same spot twice. My lieutenant stopped the column of APCs and walked up to me in the front to ask me to take over. Initially I refused to help, just for effect, because an hour ago two people with no combat experience, after being in country for a week, thought they knew it all. By this time I was senior guy in my company. After a threat and an apology, I got us to where we were supposed to be in an hour and we set up for the night. He is the same captain who was in charge a few months later when we were overrun on July 7, 1967. That captain was eventually relieved of his command.

As squad leader, I had the ability to call in air strikes, artillery, mortars and even once the SS New Jersey, the battleship built for World War II in 1942 in Philadelphia. She had 16 inch guns and they were devastating, the rounds fired from her looked like Volkswagens flying through the air. The standouts were the Air Force and Navy jet pilots we would call in for air strikes. After they were done dropping napalm or bombs, they would fly over us, fire their boosters, then turn straight up and spin. This created an after burner effect we could see, to show us they were there to support us. Of course there were always heavy duty gunship choppers to call in for help, with door-gunners and M60 machine guns and rockets on each side. The Douglas AC-47 Spooky, known among us as Puff the Magic Dragon, was a heavy, fixed wing aircraft with six barrel Gatling guns mounted underneath, capable of firing 100 rounds per second. These could devastate an area the size of a football field in two seconds. Then there was the Cessna bird dog, a lightweight, single engine aircraft with no weapons, used to spot the enemy for air strikes or to locate downed pilots. We learned that anytime you saw this light plane flying around you better get out of there fast, because there just might be an air strike soon. Other artillery or aircraft might be on the way, and friendly fire was just as dangerous as enemy fire.

Sometimes, if our artillery unit was being directly fired on, they retaliated with beehive rounds. These contained little darts called flechettes, and each round carried 8,000 of them. It was a weapon unique to the Vietnam War, fired mostly from a 155 howitzer. If an artillery unit was in danger of being overrun, they would point the cannon directly at the enemy and fire the round. It would go about 75 meters and then explode, sending darts everywhere. It would make enemy soldiers look like pin cushions, very effective, very scary. Seeing those bodies would affect you for the rest of your life. The memory of seeing things like that has a lot to do with PTSD. Then there was what napalm, a combustible, fuel-gel, would do to them. Bodies were burned to a crisp, and the memory of that smell never leaves you. This is the life of a low level Grunt combat soldier. We did all the dirty work and saw everything.

The Iron Triangle was one of the places where Agent Orange, which contains the poison Dioxin, was used extensively to defoliate the jungle. It came in barrels by ship and had to be unloaded and trucked to Tan Son Nhut Air Base. The first batch of it had been unloaded very near our Cu Chi Base Camp in the early part of 1962. By the time I arrived it had been in use for about five years already, around our camp perimeter to increase visibility. Defoliation was named Operation Ranch Hand and pretty much anyone who handled it in any way was exposed to the deadly chemical. At the airport, it had to be transferred to the helicopters and low-flying planes that did the spraying. So many fellow soldiers have gotten sick and even now others are just starting to suffer the effects. We call it Triple Play. It includes heart disease, cancer and diabetes. Most got some, some got all. Some Veterans had children later on born with birth defects and unusual problems. Any of us who have not gotten sick keep wondering when and if it will get us.

And let's not forget the Vietnamese exposure to Agent Orange. It is worse for them because not only were they poisoned along with the American soldiers, but their land was contaminated with it. They suffer greatly from the same health issues, down the line to children born later with birth defects as a result of their parents having been exposed. They have to deal with this problem without having the resources that the United States has with hospitals and doctors to help our men. Who knows how many generations will be affected there?

Every day you daydream about being home and being safe, but you are still in this place where the VC are trying to kill you. It was search and destroy with firefights during the day and going out on ambush at night while trying to sleep in shifts, always guarding the perimeter. Here we are again, *A Fight For Life*. At that point in life, at 19, you don't know who you are and sometimes you don't know what you are. But every day you have to keep on going around in a circle and getting nowhere, and then a passenger jet passes over and you dream you are on it. The hope then fades and you see where you really are and reality sets in again.

For us in Vietnam, holidays just didn't happen, the day was like any other, fighting to stay alive. No matter how your family celebrated in the States, Christmas, Hanukkah, Passover, Easter, those days were like any other day for us. You miss your family and friends but nothing changes for you out in the field. Combat is what you do. All the while we knew that at home in the United States, college students and other groups were demonstrating against the war. This certainly did not help the morale of the US soldiers fighting in Southeast Asia.

When I was a kid, I used to walk downtown to Murphy's Candy Store in the Plaza and have an ice cream soda for 25 cents. Then down the street to the bakery for day old crumb buns for five cents. Back then I did not know anything else, until I had to drink water that stunk, that we needed to put tablets in just so you could stay hydrated without getting sick. Sometimes we had peppermint candies, and I would put one in my mouth before drinking so the water would seem cool. Our food was adequate at best and the C-Rations sucked. I used to sit in the field and think about home, that's when I was most vulnerable. I would see ice cream sodas floating by and dream I was at Murphy's Candy Store.

OUT ON AMBUSH

We would set up our temporary campsite for the night like a wagon train from an old TV Western. Here is a drawing that I did when we first started working on this book (picture 27). First, second, and third platoons made up the outer ring with approximately 12 APCs. The second inner ring was the mortar platoon, with three squads in three APCs (picture 28). In the center was the headquarters platoon, which included the captain and his staff, in its own APC. Also in the center was the maintenance crew platoon, in their fully equipped mechanic's track. Every night that we were out on ambush we would set up a new, temporary campsite like this to accommodate about 75 men. Each APC had a 50 caliber machine gun in the turret with someone in the TC hatch manning the weapon all night, a driver ready to move, and other members of that squad taking turns with guard duty. We would dig a hole in front of each APC to place a 60 caliber machine gun (picture 29), and we also had grenade launchers and M16 assault weapons. Occasionally, if conditions were right, after setting up for the night, we could take a few minutes to relax. Here is a picture I took of Vinny, Lowenstein, an unnamed soldier, and Sherrill on one of those rare evenings (picture 30). Then I handed my camera to Sherrill to take this picture of Lowenstein, an unnamed soldier and me (picture 31). Soldiers carried an interesting variety of personal items in their vehicles. You can see in these pictures that some of us had American style lawn chairs. Our APCs are in place behind us, our flak jackets are on the ground near us, and our weapons are ready. We had orders for that night.

At dusk, my squad of about seven men would then quietly leave the temporary campsite on foot, loaded with equipment, and walk a few miles through the jungle to set up the ambush on a VC trail. Occasionally, two squads were sent out from one location to two predetermined ambush sites. Moving through the jungle quietly was very important. The enemy could track us and booby trap and mine the area we were headed for, then open fire on us. To set up in the correct spot, we used a predetermined set of coordinates using a compass, paper map and counting steps. When we got to the location, I would call in to the artillery unit assigned for this ambush to detonate hydal bursts in the air to make sure we were in the right place. A hydal burst is an empty (no shrapnel inside) explosive round which lights up the sky at a specific height when it explodes. One of these rounds would be exploded above the exact location where we were supposed to be. They also exploded other hydal bursts at pre-selected intervals, locations and heights, so that the enemy would not know which one really pointed to our position. These were all predetermined with a unique pattern each time. We relied very much on our artillery unit to verify our location. They had the same information we had but they were firing from a stationary, relatively safe position at our temporary base camp. They could concentrate and did not have to be too concerned with weapons' fire, punji pits or stepping on mines while working with the coordinates.

At the ambush site, we first set up claymore mines, which are detonated by a blasting cap using a hand-held detonator attached to the mine with wire. Claymore mines are designed to explode in one direction. They are loaded with C4 and BBs, with a kill zone of about fifteen feet, and flare out destroying anything in front of them. We would put out three or four of these mines in front of the ambush position and set up booby traps in front of them. This was necessary because the VC could creep up and quietly turn the claymores around, facing us, and you could blow yourself up when detonating the mines. I would shorten the seven second fuse to two seconds on an M26 grenade, pull the pin, keeping the clip pressed. Then I set the claymore on top of the grenade, keeping pressure on the clip, so if they lifted it up - goodbye gook. Yes, we used that word. We would then find an open area in the jungle to wait near the actual ambush site, which made us very vulnerable to sniper fire. Our radioman could call in anytime for whatever might be needed on any particular ambush night, but I often chose to not do that. The sound of a crackling radio on an otherwise quiet night was just too dangerous.

It was just watch and wait for a VC patrol to come down the trail. You don't know what is around you, and you have to stay vigilant and quiet. Sometimes there is activity, sometimes not. If we had a hit, we would do a quick body count and quietly walk back to our temporary campsite. We would then come back in the morning in APCs to re-examine the area and retrieve any VC bodies. Sometimes, when we saw action at the ambush site, we would just stay there for the rest of the night and have APCs come out in the morning to pick us up. There were a few times that the situation became so dangerous that vehicles left our temporary campsite during the night, and came out to the ambush location to pick us up. We still left any VC bodies for the morning. We would put the bodies in body bags and call in helicopters to come and get them. I never asked what they did with the VC bodies, we had enough to think about.

We never left any equipment or trash at the site for the VC to scavenge. They were very crafty, they had to be to survive, and could turn nothing into something. Unlike the North Vietnamese regular army, which was well supplied with Russian and Chinese weapons and equipment, the VC had next to nothing to fight with. They would make bombs and booby traps out of discarded food cans and scraps of wire. Unexploded 500 pound bombs dropped by our fighter pilots, and any pieces of metal they could find became mines in the roads. They cut the bombs in half, then used the pieces of metal as plates in the roads to cover and trigger the bombs underneath. These were deadly and could blow up our APCs and Jeeps. We were careful to never discard unused ammunition, because in those early years some of our bullets could be made to fit into their weapons.

We went out on ambush two to three times a week. This unfortunate night we were on our way to an assigned spot in the Iron Triangle, once again counting steps, while relying on a map and compass. When we were about halfway there we were attacked and we hit the dirt, all seven of us. I sent three men to the left flank, three men to the right, I stayed in the middle. We threw grenades and opened up on them with automatic weapons. After maybe a ten minute firefight everything became quiet. We radioed in to base camp and were told to abandon the ambush and come back. In the morning, we revisited the location and saw that it was a South Korean Outpost that we did not know about, and obviously they did not know that we were going to be there. The South Koreans were allies fighting with the United States and we killed them all. Maybe we were just better equipped that night or maybe we were just faster. The firefight that night could have easily gone the other way. I called in to headquarters and reported what had happened. Supervisors came out to the scene that morning and questioned me. I explained that they had opened up on us first. They understood that we just did not have any information about allies being there. Choppers were sent out that same morning to retrieve the bodies so that they could be returned to the South Korean Army. It is 2023 and I still think about what happened that night.

It was a quiet morning near the Mekong River and we had just come off all night LP (listening post) duty. I was hungry and tired and had just walked away toward the shore to relieve myself. Rounds suddenly started coming toward me, zipping by my head. I hit the ground and started to look for the sniper. I crept along the bank of the river toward the sound of the firing and saw a muzzle blast in a tree. There he was. I went a little further until I had a clear line of sight, about a hundred yards away. I took my position and fired two quick bursts at him from my M16. His rifle fell, but he never hit the ground because his ankle was shackled to the tree. He was hanging upside down. I fired two more bursts and then got out of there as quickly as possible. He was not fighting because he wanted to. He had been grabbed, shackled to the tree, given a weapon, and had no choice but to defend himself. If villagers in the south were not willing to fight with the VC, they were sometimes forced to fight this way. The VC were known to forcibly conscript young teenagers.

July 6th, 1967 - We were somewhere in the Iron Triangle, on a search and destroy mission, and the day was coming to an end, but not for my men and me. We had orders to set up an ambush for that night. My friend Bill Dillehay, a permanent member of my squad, was with us that night. The location of my 1st squad that night was about a mile and a half north of our temporary base camp. Our 3rd squad, under the command of my friend Vinny, also had an ambush that night, west of ours and about a mile from base camp. Both squads had come out of our same temporary campsite which had about 70 men, not including the two squads that had been sent out overnight. Everything was quiet that night, until about 5am on the morning of July 7th. We started to hear activity, and my radioman got a call from the campsite saying, "Help we are getting hit hard." The 3rd squad's ambush site had been closer to our temporary base camp, they heard the explosions and gunfire before they got the call and had already started back. We grabbed our gear and rushed back as well. When we got close we saw VC everywhere inside the perimeter. I got my men in through the crossfire successfully, right behind the other squad. I immediately got on the radio and called in the helicopter gunships and medevacs. There was no way for me to know if anyone else had already called in reinforcements. We and the VC had dead and wounded everywhere. We all took positions to fight back. I climbed onto my APC and started firing non-stop at the VC from the TC hatch with the mounted 50 caliber machine gun. My weapon turned red hot and I could see the rounds going through the barrel. We had special asbestos gloves used to change barrels when they got this hot, but if I stopped firing I would have been killed. The VC were all around us until the helicopter gunships arrived and they took off. The choppers chased them into the jungle and blasted the shit out of them.

I looked around and there were bodies everywhere. I saw my 1st lieutenant lying face down and turned him over, no face, no chest, he was gone. Medevac choppers came in and we loaded our wounded as fast as we could. That is when I found our maintenance chief, or what was left of him, on the ground. I went over to get him, he was still conscious but cut in half. I put him on the chopper and said, "You are going to be fine." I have regretted saying that to a dying man all my life. A number of our wounded died en route or at the hospitals, so our loss was even greater than what we originally saw. After all of our wounded were transported, all American soldiers' bodies were prepared for pick up and taken away by choppers. Then I called in Rome plows to take care of the mass grave for the dead VC soldiers. No body bags for them that day. There were no wounded VC left to deal with, we could not leave their wounded alive while we were caring for our own wounded and trying to stay alive ourselves.

That same day, while we were occupied with these clean-up tasks, battalion leaders from headquarters came out to the scene to investigate. They took statements from many of us and made the decision in the field to relieve our captain of his command. Although we knew he was incompetent, his removal was one more thing for us to process. We didn't know much about that procedure and never heard anything about him again. He was replaced with Captain William W. Hartzog, who turned out to be one hell of a military leader and a great tactician. He eventually became a 4-Star General, and we kept in touch until he passed away in 2020. During that battle I saw an amazing sight, one of our APCs had gotten hit with RPG rockets, everything inside exploded and it became a 13 ton mound of melted metal. Captain Hartzog traveled back to the area about a year later, while still on active duty, and reported that the melted APC was still there, exactly where we had left it. We had an ARVN (South Vietnamese Soldier who was supposed to be on our side) with us that day inside the perimeter. During the horrendous carnage in our temporary base camp he remained unharmed. To this day I think he gave away our location and that is how we got hit so hard and so fast. He was found dead the next day. No one asked any questions.

Another night I was on LP along the Mekong River. There were two of us on duty, armed with our M16s and grenades. Our job was to listen for the enemy and to protect our campsite. It was a quiet night so we took turns sleeping a little. Morning broke and I had to take a dump so I walked quietly to a place where I could dig a hole, and found myself face-to-face with a VC doing the same thing. We just looked at each other. He had a rifle by his side facing down, I had my M16. We kind of knew that if either one of us lifted a weapon we would both be dead. I let him back away slowly and disappear into the jungle, and I waited to do my business in a safer place. The experience of seeing that VC there was something out of this world. How we did not try to kill each other is a mystery. Every once in a while that dream still comes to me. I wake up startled every time. It was another one of those moments that just stays with you.

One day we were stopped on Highway One, which stretched north from Saigon, in our APCs with the back hatches down so we could just walk in and out. We were taking a break to eat and relieve ourselves. It was called a Highway but it was just a wide, mud trail, there was not much pavement in this primitive place. I was in the lead vehicle as usual, or point as we called it, and on this day there were maybe 20 APCs behind me. Some children came up to the back of our APC begging for food, which happened all the time. Not only were they hungry, but they knew we often had treats like fruit cocktail and candy. We would usually give them something. I tossed a can of fruit cocktail to one of them and it seemed to hit him near the top of his eye, or maybe he just pretended that it did. As that happened an old man and a child started walking toward us. I was sitting on top of my APC when I noticed that the old man was walking funny. Very quickly the kid went behind him, the old man bent down and he had a 30 caliber machine gun strapped to his back. The kid started firing at us. One of my men was in the TC hatch behind our 50 caliber machine gun eating some C-rations when this started to happen. My guy opened up and killed both of them before they did any damage. None of us got hit, thank God, but we always had to be on alert. It's *A Fight For Life*, and killing an old man and a kid makes you *Less Than A Hero*.

I was there in the early years of the war, and we could sometimes fool the enemy with simple military maneuvers, just because they had never seen those things done before. Our unit had a patrol of about 25 men stranded in the delta, in the rice paddies, and we were ordered to fly out on choppers to pick them up. Five choppers were sent out, my squad of seven men was on one of them, and the others were empty except for the pilots and door-gunners. I remember it had been raining hard and everything was soaked and muddy. It was late in the afternoon, and the patrol was waiting for us in the paddies, in front of the tree line. We suspected that we were being observed. When we landed and the 25 men split up and headed to the five choppers, my squad of seven men got off, mingled with them, and slipped into the woods near the tree line, staying behind. When the choppers took off we heard small arms fire from the VC shooting at them, but they got away clean. We then set up our ambush about 300 yards from the chopper landing zone with the usual claymore mines and two 60 caliber machine guns. The night went on, five of us staying awake, two sleeping, switching on and off till morning. I always tried to stay awake all night. We were hidden very well, anticipating that part of that same VC patrol would come to scavenge the landing zone to see if our men left anything useful. We were right, it was just getting light out when I heard movement in the jungle. A couple of twig crackling sounds meant someone was walking near the ambush. As soon as they crossed in front I gave the signal to open up with everything. We detonated the claymores, riddled them with the 60 caliber machine guns, and in seconds they were all dead. Mission accomplished very well, but we knew we had given away our position. I had my radioman call in to our temporary campsite, and we were advised to find a spot and camp for the night. There were too many enemy patrols in the area to chance having a chopper come in right away. We gathered all of our equipment and trash, and started moving as quickly as we could. We had just started to walk away from the bodies, when one of my men started cutting an ear off one of the dead VC soldiers, thinking he would get one from each body. As squad leader, I did not tolerate desecrating a body, so I kicked him to the ground as he was crouching over the dead soldier. I told him, "You don't do that shit on my patrol, and if we don't get the hell out of here fast, we will be the dead bodies on the ground." He made a scene, but I was squad leader and gave the orders. The VC were soldiers and deserved respect. If he wanted to be a big shot with ears around his neck, he would have to do it somewhere else, not on my watch. We hurried off into the thick jungle to set up camp for the night and stayed hidden and alert until morning, when I could safely radio in for a chopper to pick us up. We were lucky to not run into any more VC because we were out of claymores and had used up most of our ammo the night before. Also, we did not know if the soldiers we had killed were part of a bigger, well organized unit, or if there were solitary snipers or small patrols in the area. The next morning, before we called a chopper to pick us up, I decided to call in some artillery using the coordinates from the day before. I ordered in a hydal burst to accurately pinpoint our location, and then ordered a volley of fire in the area around us. Everything went well. I will never know if they hit anyone or anything that morning. If anyone had been there, at least we scared them away. Two Hueys came in to pick us up. In a dangerous situation like this, even though only one chopper was needed, they often sent two. When we were waiting in a jungle clearing like that, with all the equipment we had with us, it was quicker and safer with two. The choppers landed, we loaded and took off without incident. My squad made it back to our field base camp safely, none of my men wounded or killed, and twelve enemy soldiers dead. No souvenir ears were taken.

One night, after being out on search and destroy all day, we were scheduled for an ambush that night. A German Shepherd and handler had been with us during the day and the decision was made for them to stay with our squad overnight. I proceeded to verify the proper ambush location in the usual way, coordinating with the artillery unit assigned to protect us.

Usually, when the hydal bursts are set off at the proper altitude, the pieces scattered harmlessly in a wide circle around us. Even though it is a non-explosive round, it is still a metal sphere that breaks apart. On this night, a mistake was made and one of them was set off too low to the ground. A falling piece hit and killed the dog and his handler was injured. I called in to report this friendly fire incident and to request an APC to transport the handler and the body of his dog. The handler was not badly injured so we did not need a chopper. We were ordered to evacuate the ambush site and return to our temporary base camp for the night. It was fortunate that no VC heard or reacted to this commotion. The next day we returned to Cu Chi Base Camp and the loyal dog had a proper burial there.

Having to set up these ambushes and wait all night is bad enough, but in a torrential downpour it's much, much worse. First of all it is hot, but you still have to wear a poncho to try and stay dry and for protection against mosquitoes, with the flak vest under the poncho for protection. Snakes and mosquitoes especially liked that rainy weather at night. This particular night we were trudging along in the heavy rain trying to reach our ambush site by counting steps. I don't know whether it is harder to keep quiet when the ground is dry or wet. We were seven men, the usual squad count, moving along slowly and carefully. I had an uneasy feeling that we were being followed or watched. We were always in danger of being hit from the back or sides as we moved along in a line. I signaled everyone by holding up my hand, to stop and take a listening position. I was sure the VC were close by, so I gave another hand signal to get ready to fire if necessary. Sure enough, I heard more sounds, and before they could surround us, I had everyone open fire in the direction of the noise. We heard screams, some of them must have been hit, and they must have retreated because we didn't hear anything else for a while. It was too dangerous that night to go back and look for bodies. I decided to abandon the ambush and try to get back to our temporary base camp, which was set up in an open field near the city of Tay Ninh. We started to move, but I sensed that whoever was out there was not through with us. We radioed in that we were coming back, that we had been ambushed ourselves with no wounded or casualties at the moment. I heard noise again, this time in front of us, so we stopped and I decided to set up our ambush right there because going forward might get us all killed. We set up our 60 caliber machine gun aimed toward where we heard the noise, got down in the mud, and waited. Our ponchos had protected us somewhat but the mosquitoes were now inside our clothing and biting. For the rest of the night we did not go beyond our barrier of claymores, small arms set-up and machine guns, and it remained quiet. Morning came, the rain had stopped, and whatever bodies might have been in the area were gone. It was probably a small patrol, not well armed, and I do not know how much damage we did to them. I could not use the radio to call in because we were no longer in the location of our scheduled ambush, and the noise could get us killed with friendly fire. We set our sights on quietly walking back to our base camp in the field to get dry, get some breakfast and rest. It had been an exhausting night. We got back safely.

Waiting all night for something to happen is awful. The enemy knew the jungle better than we ever could. They were everywhere and could pop out of tunnels or come out of the tree line anytime. You shoot at anyone that walks in front of you, then take a body count and get the hell out of there. Sometimes the pressure just got to us. I was out there with six men, and they depended on me. These were long nights, and you had to stay awake if you wanted to stay alive. First we had to secure the perimeter, then everyone had to pull guard duty at night in three hour shifts. My technique was to burn my fingers, that would certainly keep you up. They gave out speed and methedrine pills if you wanted them. It was bad enough just being out in that cursed jungle, everyone drank and smoked pot. There were a few nights when we would go out and not set up the scheduled ambush, just stay hidden and quiet in the jungle overnight. I would not feel right about this and was afraid of getting caught, but we just needed a night off. For at least those few nights, I kept my men safe.

The Vietnamese were defending their own country and somebody was always invading it. First Japan in World War II, then the French exploited them, then their own civil war between the North and the South, and then the US got involved. They got the Japanese out, they got the French out, and eventually they got the US out.

Picture 1 - Soldier with equipment.

Picture 2 - Supply Building at base camp.

Picture 3 - Frank with mail in his hand.

Picture 4 - Soldiers walking past sign near perimeter.

Picture 5 - Explosions outside perimeter seen from base camp.

Picture 6 - Richie standing outside perimeter in cleared area.

Picture 7 - Soldiers sitting on sandbag bunker.

Picture 8 - Richie sitting on sandbag bunker with weapon.

Picture 9 - Area outside perimeter cleared with Agent Orange.

Picture 10 - Richie posing on mechanic's track with pet dog.

Picture 11 - Richie on mechanic's track showing boom.

Picture 12 - Soldiers posing with base camp sign.

Picture 13 - Richie posing at sign with pet dog.

Picture 14 - Soldier with guitar standing near Jeep.

Picture 15 - Knox with pet monkey.

Picture 16 - Sherrill at base camp with two other soldiers.

Picture 17 - Sherrill standing near perimeter with Knox.

Picture 18 - Vinny, standing just outside the perimeter.

Picture 19 - Bad Brad standing next to his
damaged APC, Mellow Yellow.

Picture 20 - Richie posing with Brad's damaged APC.

Picture 21 - Another squad getting ready to move out.

Picture 22 - Soldiers covering their ears during mortar firing.

Picture 23 - Sandstorm at base camp.

Picture 24 - Burned out hut in the jungle.

Picture 25 - Richie standing next to rusted
girder on Michelin property.

Picture 26 - Explosion behind APC, across the field.

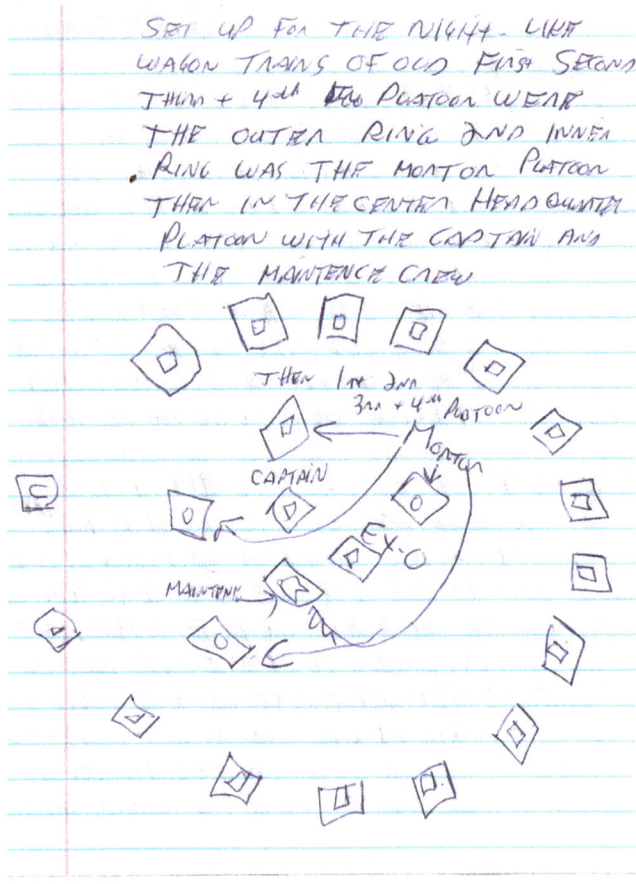

Picture 27 - Richie's drawing of temporary base camp set-up.

Picture 28 - APCs set up in temporary base camp.

Picture 29 - Richie digging hole in front
of APC for M60 machine gun.

Picture 30 - Vinny, Lowenstein, unnamed soldier, Sherrill.

Picture 31 - Lowenstein, unnamed soldier, Richie.

Picture 32 - Stewardess on R&R flight.

Picture 33 - Woman who Richie was friendly with in Singapore.

Picture 34 - Richie in front of tailor store in Singapore.

Picture 35 - Family home of woman friend in Singapore.

Picture 36 - Richie arriving at Bangkok Airport for R&R.

Picture 37 = A woman friend of Richie's in Bangkok.

Picture 38 - Richie and another soldier ready to come home.

Picture 39 - Richie and another soldier laughing, waiting for bus.

Picture 40 - Richie and Bill Dillehay in Florida in 2024.

Picture 41 - Bill and Jane Dillehay in Florida in 2024.

Picture 42 - Dennis Reilly, Monica, Richie and Kathy in 2021.

R & R

During a one year deployment, everyone was supposed to get two, separate, one week R&Rs, and one three day in country R&R leave. These trips would be to a country of your choice from an approved list. R&R allocations came up once a month for a few members of each battalion on a rotating schedule. However, sometimes an individual on the list did not want to go at that time or did not have enough money. So as to not lose the allotment, someone else could go instead. Frank would often get this information first and ask me if I wanted to go in that person's place. That is how I got to go on three, one week R&Rs. In order to go you had to have $300 dollars to make sure that you could pay for the hotel rooms and everything else you wanted. That rule, and the transportation, were set up by the Army and no one left for R&R without $300. The money was never a problem for me, I had my poker winnings to spend. There were a few places to choose from, and my first choice was TaiPei, Taiwan. We flew out of Tan Son Nhut Airbase in a

1950s Pan Am prop plane, off to a country I had never heard of. I remember that first night, sleeping in my hotel room, without having to worry about getting killed, and that was beautiful.

The next day, we dressed in civilian clothes and went to a bar where the girls were, and I really needed a girl. There were lots of pretty young girls, and all you had to do was pick one. First you had to buy three drinks for you and the girl you liked. Whiskey and Coke was the drink of choice, and although I did not know it at the time, the girls' drinks were usually just plain Coke or tea. After choosing the girl and buying the drinks, it was $15 a day, and I signed a contract. The agreement was that I would not hurt her and would pay all expenses for the time we were together, or be arrested and jailed. I spoke to a few girls and picked one. I don't remember her name but she was pretty and sweet and for whatever time you had with them they acted like your girlfriend. The first thing we did was go back to my hotel and have sex, beautiful sweet sex like she loved me my whole life. I was with her for two days. This was a new experience for me, and I wanted to then spend time with a different girl. When I went back to the bar to pick another girl, the first one saw me and called me a butterfly for wanting someone else. She said this with a friendly smile, it was just a term they used for soldiers who switched girls. This second girl was a disappointment to me, she looked great, like they all did, but when we got to my hotel room she removed fake eyelashes, a wig, false breasts and looked older. I was only 19 and had no idea about such things. They were all sweet and personable and would do anything I wanted.

My hotel room in Taipei had a small balcony and an adjoining room with double doors that locked from each side. My fourth morning there I stepped out onto the balcony and met two girls who were on the balcony of the adjoining room and started talking to them. A sergeant, who had already paid for the company of those two girls, was in that room, passed out drunk. They couldn't leave, they were bored, and I had pot and alcohol to offer them. I had bought the local pot, known as tai sticks, from a hotel employee. It came in American paper coin rollers and was in chunks, more like hash, and it was smoked in a pipe. I guess they liked me and what I had to offer, because they asked if I would like to spend some time with them. I didn't want to go into that officer's room, so we unlocked both doors and they came into my room for the afternoon. I had sex with both girls, and they would not accept money from me because they had already been paid for the time. Very lucky for me that the sergeant never woke up during our activities. That was a lot for one afternoon and I remember that I just relaxed in my hotel room that evening. I was only in Taipei for one week, so my romances were short lived. It was my first R&R experience and I will never forget it. Then back to the wet jungle I went.

My next trip, a few months later, to Singapore, was my most memorable R&R experience. Again, a group of us from different platoons flew out on an old prop plane. Well, the landing gear of that plane failed to deploy, and they were unsuccessful in trying to lower it manually. Then we heard, "Brace for impact." All of us soldiers were thinking the same thing, *I can't believe I survived fighting in the jungles of Vietnam only to be killed in this plane crash.* Our pilots and ground crew were not going to let that happen. They lined the entire landing strip with foam and the plane belly-landed and skidded on that foam for what felt like forever. There were no injuries. Here is one of the stewardesses (that is what flight attendants were called in the 60s) from that flight, posing for my camera (picture 32).

Singapore was the cleanest city I have ever seen in my life. A lot of people from India lived there and sacred cows roamed the streets. United States currency at the time was worth three times its face value. Here the women were only $12 a day. I went to a bar and chose a sweet, great looking girl, and had to sign the usual contract and buy three drinks, just like before. Back to my hotel room for sex, then we went out to eat. She knew the city well, and that evening took me to another hotel with an elevator that opened onto the roof which had a large dance floor and bar. We spent time there drinking and dancing. In any of these establishments the music was always American soul music like The Temptations or The Four Tops. Then she took me to a casino. I gave her some gambling money and she won what was surely a lot of money to her, but she would not keep it, and insisted on giving me her winnings. The next day, I took her shopping, bought her some nice clothes and gifts, and ordered a tailor-made suit for myself. Here she is, in front of that tailor shop (picture 33). Then a store employee took this picture of me in the same spot (picture 34). Later, we went in a rickshaw to visit her parents, who lived in a small house just outside of the city. They were proud of their home, and were pleased when I asked if I could take a picture of it (picture 35). I bought some amazing local pot from them. It was unusual with the sticks and buds still mixed in, wrapped and skewered on a stick like a cigar. My God it was good, and we went back to town and rode around in a rickshaw, smoking pot and fooling around. I never got in trouble, but there were strict drug laws and I am lucky I did not get caught. I learned that in Singapore the women working in the bars at night had other jobs during the day, and the one I was with was a school teacher. Being in the sex trade in Singapore when I was there was not looked down upon. These women were treated with respect, and her parents seemed to like me. It was a way to bring extra money into the household.

It was still my Singapore week and some soldiers in a bar told me about an extraordinary place they had been to, right over the border of Singapore into Malaysia. American soldiers were not legally allowed there, so I had to ride in the trunk of a cab both ways. It was an incredible place with many beautiful girls to pick from. A woman servant, dressed like the other girls, walked around with a cart filled with all different liquors to choose from, and pot and uppers and downers, whatever you wanted. It cost about $50 for the night, including everything. We were told that the girls there received regular medical care, including testing for STDs. I chose a girl, and what a night it was. She was amazing and again would do anything. It was a way for us to temporarily forget the horrors of war. After what felt like the best week of my life, it was time to go back to the jungle.

My third official R&R was to Bangkok, Thailand. A fellow soldier who was on my plane took this picture of me at the airport when we first arrived (picture 36). Everything about the bars and the girls and the rules was similar to Taipei and Singapore. The dance clubs and bars catered to American servicemen. Here is one of the women who kept me company on this trip, they were always happy to pose for my camera (picture 37). The jukebox would be loaded with the same American music, but the mechanism was different from the ones in the States. There was a screen inside, behind the turntable, and when the record dropped and the song started playing, a projector would show the group on the screen singing the song. While the record played we watched what were probably the first music videos. For everyone too young to know, in the States, you just saw the vinyl record drop and the arm came down and the song was played.

For my 3 day in-country leave I went to the ocean city of Vung Tau, a beautiful seaside location with a big beach and signs everywhere about strong rip tides. I spent most of the time relaxing on the beach. The sex trade here was not established and controlled like the other places I had visited. Here it was more like the horse stalls that were in the Vietnam countryside, where you had sex on beds of hay. The women for sale here, and the situation, did not seem safe so I had this three day leave without that type of female companionship. There were many bars, restaurants and shops catering to servicemen and it was a favorite destination for our in country trips. Games of chance with cards or dice were everywhere and I gambled a lot. There were rumors that Vietnamese soldiers also used this city to temporarily escape the war. Something unusual that I remember, there were beautifully dressed women walking around and we were told not to approach them. They were just there to stroll around to make the area look pleasant and inviting. It worked, they were great to look at. Vung Tau is still a destination for many in that part of the world who just want to get away to a beach town for a while.

So strange to have these R&R trips and then go right back to the jungle, fighting for my life.

WOUNDED

One morning, I woke up at our temporary campsite with a terrible pain in my upper left thigh. We had been in a firefight the day before with a large group of VC. They were firing mortars and I realized that I must have gotten hit by shrapnel. I did not feel it happen, but there was a big, raised wound on my leg. Walking on it hurt too much, so I requested to go back to base to see a doctor. A chopper was sent out for me and I was taken to our 12th Evac Hospital in Cu Chi. I had been in that hospital briefly during my first weeks in country to have a cyst removed.

The history and evolution of the 12th Evacuation Hospital was a favorite topic of conversation among the staff and patients. It was formed in 1917 in the United States, and moved to France during World War I, as a main battlefield hospital and officially named the 12th Evacuation Hospital. It was dissolved after World War I but brought back in 1925. In 1943 the hospital was reactivated and sent to Europe for World War II. In those days the hospital complex was smaller and consisted of tents. Then in 1966 it was reinvented again and sent to Cu Chi Base Camp in Vietnam. It belonged to the 25th Infantry, my unit, for the duration of the war, built over the largest enemy tunnel complex in Vietnam. I spent 4-5 weeks there.

The hospital area was a series of permanent Quonset huts with air conditioning. Local women were employed here also to clean and do laundry. There was a raised landing area for choppers at the end of the rows of huts, and the first hut nearest the landing zone was for triage. Sometimes, if the wounded started coming in quickly, they would triage right at the chopper landing pad. One hut was specially equipped for surgery. Most of the huts were for recovering soldiers and were set up with twenty cots each in two orderly rows. There were wires, generators and back-up generators everywhere. Doctors removed the piece of shrapnel from my thigh and stitched up the wound. I spent a few days rolling around in my wheelchair on the hospital grounds and I saw a lot of wounded coming in. Speed was everything. Orderlies would race to the choppers, remove the stretchers, put them on gurneys and wheel them into the triage hut. These choppers had what we called sleds on each side, to carry the stretchers, and sometimes they carried more wounded men in the cab. This meant that sometimes five or more would come in together. When there was a firefight our pilots would bring them in, unload, and then fly back out to pick up more. Sometimes this went on for hours until the firefight was over. If the chopper was going back, usually with a turn-around time of a few minutes, the stretcher was replaced.

If they were not going back out, the pilots returned the chopper to the airbase at Cu Chi, parked it, and stayed at base camp until they were called out again. Warrant Officer was the rank of most pilots, and they were permanently assigned to our Cu Chi Base Camp just like us Grunts.

Medics were always out in the field with us and in constant danger just like combat soldiers. They carried a medical supply backpack and other supplies, including morphine, and were specially trained for what they had to do. For catastrophic wounds, where internal organs were exposed, they would put the body parts, still attached to the body, into a plastic bag and transport the soldier with the bag. Putting internal organs back into a hole in the body out in the jungle would result in a fatal infection. They saved many lives. Some of them were medics by choice and carried weapons, and some were conscientious objectors who refused to touch weapons. The CIs were drafted like the rest of us, and somewhere along the line were given this choice. They were not automatically made officers like other medical personnel. Some conscientious objectors became cooks.

Most of our doctors were young, and some were inexperienced with battlefield wounds. I saw some of our soldiers come in alive but ripped to shreds. If they were gone from the waist down from tripping on mines, they would just administer morphine and let them die. I heard a few dying boys ask for their mother, most of us did not have wives yet. The staff only worked on the ones they thought they could save. Decisions had to be made. A few times I heard doctors ask guys who had no legs or other horrific injuries if they wanted to be saved, giving them the opportunity to make a choice. Imagine being 19 years old and having to make that choice,

When you entered the hut with the recovering wounded, the smell of the soldiers who were amputees was overwhelming. I can still remember that smell. Sometimes, depending on how many were there at any given time, the amputees were in a separate hut. The situation in our hospital was not conducive to anyone's healing. The VC would take a position in the jungle just outside the hospital perimeter and randomly fire mortars at the area. We would have to lie on the floor with our mattresses on top of us. I don't remember anything hitting the building that I was in while I was there, but we all had to cover ourselves when the firing started. For soldiers who were not able to cover themselves, the staff did their best to protect them, while trying to stay alive.

In my recovery hut, across from me and two beds over, was a seriously wounded VC soldier with IVs and tubes. He was already there when I was assigned a cot in that hut and I don't know why he was there. He was the only VC soldier I ever saw being treated in our hospital. Wounded enemy personnel being brought back to our hospital was unheard of. The next day, when I woke up, I saw that all his tubes had been ripped out and a doctor came in and pronounced him dead. There were no questions about this, no investigation was done, and that was the end of it.

My wound was not healing. I was told that the lymph node in my groin had become infected and had to be removed. So into the operating room I went, and woke up in one of the

Quonset huts to supposedly begin my recovery from that surgery. What a horror that turned out to be. I was so sick from whatever they used to put me to sleep that I couldn't sit up or eat without vomiting. They gave me morphine intravenously for the pain. One morning I was feeling so sick I just could not wake up. The nurse who was trying to wake me got very impatient and dumped water on my face. A doctor saw her, came over, and shouted, "How dare you throw water in a combat soldier's face." The nurse was a captain, and the doctor documented a reprimand which resulted in her losing one of her stripes, demoting her from captain to lieutenant. That lower rank meant lower pay and loss of some privileges, plus having the reprimand on her permanent record.

After about three days I could sit up in a wheelchair again and go outside and watch the choppers come in with wounded. The medical evac choppers were manned just like the ones in combat, a pilot and co-pilot for insurance, and door-gunners for protection. This particular morning, I saw a chopper coming in awkwardly. It was tilting back and forth and I could see that there were wounded men on both sleds. They somehow got it down and shut it off. The co-pilot was already dead, probably from small arms fire. The pilot died a few minutes later while they were taking the wounded off. I tried to find out but never learned what happened to the wounded soldiers that they sacrificed their lives for.

That same day, another chopper came in, and I watched the attendees put the wounded soldier on a gurney to wheel him into the triage room as quickly as possible. There were poles outside the huts holding up tarps for shade and they ran into one of the poles. The wounded soldier went flying and hit the ground rolling. They quickly picked him up, put him back onto the gurney, and just kept going. I learned later that he survived and was sent home.

I saw so many men come in with horrific wounds. I have a special place in my soul for all Vietnam Veterans, but especially the wounded soldiers. I remember going to visit one of our men who had stepped on a mine, a black kid who was barely 19, a friend of mine and a great guy. Before I became a sergeant I used to go to the enlisted men's club with him to drink and dance and forget the war for a brief time. I do not remember his name. Both of his legs were gone up to his testicles. He loved to dance, it was really hard to see him like that. But who else was going to visit him? He just said to me, "How am I going to dance? How can I face my girlfriend? I just want to die." Two days later he passed away. It was very sad for me. We used to listen to The Temptations and The Four Tops on the jukebox and do the Boogaloo. My heart sank, another boy killed.

When my parents learned that I was in the hospital, that is when they found out I had been in combat all along. I started to write honest letters to them about my experiences. Before I came home they destroyed those letters. I have to go by memory and what my friend Frank tells me went on during my recovery. After a few more days they released me back to my unit for light duty. The next day I started feeling sick and my stitches were opening up, so back to the hospital I went. They had to open up the wound and restitch it. I did not know what was going to happen next. I was back in the wheelchair, rolling around the grounds of the 12th Evac again.

My wound still wasn't healing. I developed a fever of 105, and they even tried putting me on an ice blanket in an effort to lower the fever. Right there at the hospital was what was called a Mars Station, a way for us to call home in extreme situations and I was approved to use it. It is a phone that called an Army station in the Philippines, and in turn they would somehow relay the call to who you wanted to talk to in the States. Remember it was 1967 and we still had rotary phones. I spoke to my mom and told her the situation with my leg and how it was not healing. She said she would call our senators for help and she did. This saved my life, who else but your mother, right? A few days later, an experienced, older doctor flew into Cu Chi from Saigon. He walked in, saw my leg, got a scalpel, stabbed my wound, and blue and green pus and blood gushed out. It was gangrene. He said to the younger doctors, "You cannot sew up this type of wound like that, you have to clean it, leave it open, and let it heal on its own." There was a hole in my leg and they used something on the wound to keep the skin growth even. Today I have a large, sunken scar.

Somewhere along the way I was in a coma, of course I did not know it. According to my buddy Frank, who visited me every day, the coma lasted for three days. Thanks to this doctor and my mother, I lived and went back to fight another day.

My time spent in the 12th Evac was rough but it was safer than being out in the field. During my recuperation, I was grateful to be away from the fighting and to be able to rest and sleep. I was better off than most of the soldiers there. I again spent time rolling around in my wheelchair visiting different guys to help cheer them up. Talking about home, what we called the *world*, always helped everyone. The subject was often about what you were going to do with your life when you got home, knowing that a lot of us would not see home again. Doughnut Dollies were always visiting the wounded.

It was during this stay in the hospital that I met Charlton Heston. I was sitting up in my bed, still recuperating from the surgery and the effects of the anesthesia. They told us that a movie star was at the hospital to visit the wounded. He walked in there like a general and stopped at my cot. He said, "How are you doin' soldier?" I was still in a daze from the powerful pain medications, and at first I thought it was either God or Moses. He spoke to me as if he had known me my whole life and I said, "Wow my mother will not believe this, she adores you." He said, "Thank God for your mother, I could not be successful without people like her." Then he took a card out of his case and wrote her a note. I remember it saying something like *I am sitting here with your son, a great soldier, who has done his country a great service without hesitation. I am privileged to have met him. He is doing fine, may God bless him and your whole family*, signed Charlton Heston. That was a monumental moment for me to remember for the rest of my life. For him to take the time to come to a country at war and risk his life, just to make some soldiers feel better, showed me how much some people cared about us. He spoke to many of us about young men putting their lives on the line. I mailed the card to my mother and it made her so happy to know I was doing better, and that her favorite actor had come to see me. I believe she kept the card until she entered a nursing home at 95 years old. Like many other things, we could not locate it among her belongings. I learned later that Charlton Heston was a World War II Veteran and had visited our wounded troops in Vietnam several times.

While there, I became very good friends with a Peruvian male nurse. He was a big sweetheart of a guy who had become an American citizen and then been drafted. He always said he would connect with me back in the States, and when his tour was over, he did. He visited me in Teaneck, and brought me a big chunk of hash from one of his Peruvian contacts, along with a pipe he had made from a trumpet. My friends and I smoked that hash in that trumpet pipe, and one of my friends who was there that night still has the trumpet pipe.

I spent a lot of time talking to the doctors, nurses and attendants and learned a lot about them. They talked about how our military began drafting doctors with little or no warning to serve in Vietnam. They had to go through basic training, learn officer protocol, and how to handle firearms. Even though they were already doctors, the most important thing was to learn battlefield surgery. When they were drafted they did not have that experience and were not prepared for the horrific injuries that happen in combat. No amount of training prepared those young doctors for what they would have to do. Most of the nurses were women who enlisted right out of nursing school.

After a few days my wound began to heal properly, and I was sent back to my hooch for light duty on base camp. For me, already a sergeant, that meant supervising the filling of sandbags and other work to maintain our Ann Margret bunker system. This work was done by Vietnamese civilians, and by our guys assigned to light duty. One of the workers was a cute girl in her twenties who loved to gamble, a favorite pastime whenever we were around these civilians at our base camp. She already knew poker but wanted me to teach her Gin Rummy. She insisted on playing for money and in a few weeks she lost about $50 to me in Vietnamese money. I could spend that money locally or convert it into military payments certificates. She and I had a lot of fun playing cards, and she did not give up trying to win the money back until I went back to active duty.

Another chore that was under the heading of light duty for me was destroying defective or unusable ammunition. I had done this many times out in the field where we had plenty of room. In base camp, we would dig a hole a short distance outside of the perimeter, place a blasting cap at the bottom, and whatever needed to be blown up was placed on top of that. The blasting cap would be detonated by a hand-held device attached by a wire. We would then go back into one of the bunkers before detonating the device. This time the pieces came through that small hole in the bunker, blew me back and I hit the opposite wall. Along with it, a piece of something shot through the hole and hit me in the eye. I couldn't see out of that eye for a few days.

I received several blood transfusions during my time at our hospital. An overwhelming number of wounded soldiers were always being brought in and a lot of whole blood was used.

It was 1967, and they did not have the testing technology or the necessary information about blood-borne diseases. In 2019, one of my blood tests at the VA showed that I had Hepatitis. According to them, Hep C can lie dormant and undetectable for decades. They gave me more tests to determine exactly which strain of Hepatitis I had, and it showed that I had Hep C and not Hep B. This had to be done because, they explained, the drug to treat the C strain is often harmful if given to someone with the B strain. I had to take the drug for 84 days at the same time every day and missing a day was not an option. After 23 days I had to go in for another blood test. The virus was no longer detectable, but I had to finish the 84 day regimen. I do not remember much except that I was tired all the time and slept a lot. All alcohol was forbidden during the treatment and for several months afterward. I had my wife and children to watch over me during that difficult time. For many of us, even 50 years later, this is another health threat hanging over Vietnam Veterans.

I was cared for at the 12th Evac and my life was saved and I am grateful. So many healthy, young men lost their lives or had their lives permanently altered by amputations or disabilities. I watched this happening day after day for a month.

THE LAST STRETCH

I went to the commissary and bought a short timer's cane when I had about 30 days left on my rotation. Mine was a foot long and had the brass head of a dragon. The tradition is to carry that stick for your last 30 days so that everyone knows you have a very good chance of getting back to the States alive. This is the time when you have to be the most careful, and just being more careful means that you might be edgy and put yourself at greater risk. It is such a dangerous time, a lot of guys got killed or wounded in their last month. I remember knowing it was Christmas Day, out on search and destroy like any other day, and knowing I had 14 days left in combat. For me, it meant no more tunnels, let some other gung-ho rookies go, I did my share. I didn't feel guilty about this, I just wanted to get home with all my limbs and my life. All of the things I had to do and all the terrible things I saw were now stored in my memory forever.

My last 30 days were spent in the field, still in combat. I got back to the safety of our base camp the day before my rotation date. Your rotation date is the day you are sent back to the States to finish serving the rest of your time, usually with a safe assignment on a US base. I should have been sent back to Cu Chi Base Camp three days before my rotation date, but we had been out in the Ho Bo Woods for weeks on search and destroy and we got hit. We had been living out of our APCs while protecting a local artillery unit. I was a buck Sergeant E-5, under the command of our 1st sergeant, who was an E-8 at the time. An E-8 was a non-commissioned officer, usually someone who fought bravely alongside the soldiers, and was usually respected by Grunts and officers, all the way up to the generals. On this day, about four weeks before my rotation date, the E-8 officer in command was none of those things. Out in the jungle, while we were under attack, this E-8 ran and hid under his Jeep. We couldn't believe that this sergeant would panic and do something like that. I followed him, pulled him out and kicked him in the ass. He freaked out and changed my orders, keeping me in the field three extra days. That was a cowardly and terrible thing to do, to keep a soldier out in combat when he was scheduled to go home. He knew it, too, but he was a scum bag.

The day finally came. Here we are, waiting for the bus, with our belongings packed and ready to go home (pictures 38, 39), to be dropped off at Tan Son Nhut Airfield. I am with another soldier from my platoon, smiling and laughing at my camera at the thought of being alive and leaving. First, we were told to undress and throw all our clothing into a bin, and we were issued new uniforms. In the front of the room was a big box made of wood, about eight feet long, five feet wide and six feet high. It looked like a big coffin. A staff sergeant came into the room and announced, "No one is going to board the plane with contraband so I am going to leave the room for 20 minutes. Anything that you have that you should not have, put it in the box. You will be searched before you board the plane." I never saw anything like it in my life, duffle bags were turned upside down and dumped on the floor. Guys had grenades, AK47s, M16 machine guns, whole machine guns taken apart, mortar rounds, plastic bags full of pot, lots of ammunition and all kinds of crazy things. When they were done, the box was overflowing. The officer came back into the room and said, "Now you can go home." Nobody was searched. The fear of getting left behind was enough to make everyone dump everything into that box.

A Continental Airlines commercial jet was waiting for us, with civilian pilots and civilian stewardesses. It was January 8, 1968, the Tet Offensive had started, and the VC were attacking the airfield with bombs and small arms fire. That civilian crew was as brave as could be, but we were unarmed and could not defend ourselves or them. We all boarded anyway, and the pilot came on the loudspeaker and asked, "Do you want to get off the plane and wait or should we go now?" Everyone screamed "Go" and off we went in what was referred to as the Freedom Bird. We refueled somewhere in the Pacific and landed at Edwards Air Force Base in California. I was back in the USA and I kissed the ground, a lot of us getting off the plane did that. Then it was off to LAX for a flight to Newark, NJ on another commercial jet. I had certainly done a lot of flying in the past year on prop planes, jets and helicopters in combat, but now being in the air felt safe. There would be no more search and destroy missions, no more ambushes and no more tunnels, thank God. I had a 30 day leave coming, with pay, plenty of cash to spend and a brand new 1968 Pontiac GTO waiting for me in my driveway. I had planned to catch a cab to Teaneck after landing in Newark. My travel pay allotment was a good amount of money, way more than I needed to get home.

As I walked through the airport in California in my uniform some people cursed at me. When I got to Newark, I was walking through the airport to get my duffle bag and find a cab, and people started yelling at me. One guy called me "baby killer." After being called names I got spit on. They did not seem to be demonstrating or waiting for returning soldiers, they looked like they just happened to be there and reacted. I could not believe it. I just kept going because at this point I thought if I got into a fight I might kill someone. I knew how to do it without a weapon. We knew there had been unrest at home over the war but I didn't think they would take it out on me. I had been drafted and did what I had been asked to do. I would never have run off to Canada. In my mind that would have been cowardly.

I got into a cab and headed home. At the time I didn't realize how tan I was from all those days in the sun. When I arrived at my parents' house there were *Welcome Home* signs everywhere, but my mother and grandmother didn't recognize me at first. My dad was at work and arrived to greet me a few hours later. After some hugs and a home cooked meal, I changed into civvies and went out the back door to my new car. I was as excited as could be.

I was home from Nam and had some time to spend with my family and my girlfriend, Gale, a beautiful girl with long blond hair. She was in Lavalette at the Jersey Shore, on vacation with her family. I rented a room there for a few days. I had met her when I was 17 and she was 15, now I was 19 and she was 17. She had written to me all the while, and although her letters were full of love, she was immature and could never understand what I had been through. I had changed, she was the same girl. Spending time with her again did not work out very well. We never had sex. When that relationship ended, even though we knew we were not meant for each other, I cried. I never saw her again, she eventually married and had five children. I recently learned that she died in 2000 of lung cancer, even though she never smoked anything in her life. She grew up in a small house in Bergenfield, NJ with a family of smokers. My first girlfriend, I still think about her.

I had exchanged letters with many girls who had written to me in Nam, and I decided to contact and maybe visit or date some of them. I was no longer a virgin, was well built, had bought some new clothes, had the mod look with long hair, a new car and money to spend. I was very confident and having sexual relationships with them came easily to me. I went to see my old friends, especially my high school friend John, who had written to me all the while. He introduced me to the serious drugs he had been doing. I still had six months left in the Army, so during that 30 day leave I tried to keep the drug use at a minimum and stay out of trouble. An honorable discharge was important.

For my remaining time, I was stationed at Fort Knox in Kentucky, in charge of what the army called the pol dumps, the gas and diesel filling station on the base. Since I had civilians working for me, I just let them do their jobs. I would stop in every once in a while to check on them or call in to see if I was needed. I did not even have to report for roll call, so I got a room in the local Holiday Inn and ate well. I bought a horse and boarded him at a local stable where he was fed and taken care of for a monthly fee. It was great to go riding on the local mountain trails and I kept him for the rest of my time in Kentucky. I had my GTO with me and I would drive soldiers back and forth to the airport, charging them less than a cab would have. Then off I would go to Churchill Downs to bet on horses or go looking for girls. For a while, I was dating two sisters and neither of them knew about the other. That could not go on for long and eventually became a problem. I fooled around with a lot of women, once getting caught with the sheriff's wife in my back seat. She was always dressed provocatively around the servicemen, flirting and showing off her legs in a mini skirt. I was arrested, taken to jail, hosed down and beaten. They knew how to do it without leaving any marks. After a while, they called my company commander and he came to pick me up and drove me back to my car. He was laughing about what had happened but I wasn't, I was still in pain from the beatdown. There were a lot of other women too, why not?

Life at Fort Knox was good. It was also the beginning of my slide into serious drug use. Even though we smoked pot and drank in Nam, it was never excessive. We needed to stay sharp in combat. At Fort Knox, I started doing cough medicine Robitussin AC with codeine and it produced a real nice rush. There was a drug store off base that sometimes had a line to buy this and he always sold to us. I don't know how the druggist didn't get in trouble for selling all that cough medicine. I drank and smoked pot with the cough medicine, and we called that combination Robo, a lot of servicemen I knew there were doing it. I found out where to get other drugs in the black part of town. I would buy uppers called Christmas Trees and Black Beauties and I was taking a lot of them. By 1968 the race riots had started, even in Kentucky, but I would calmly go to that part of town to get drugs. They were looting stores, starting fires and turning over police cars, but they never bothered outsiders coming in to buy drugs. It was business as usual for them.

I received my honorable discharge on July 3, 1968 and drove home to New Jersey in my GTO.

POST TRAUMATIC
STRESS DISORDER

We referred to being back home in the United States as being *back in the world*. Then, years later, after being *back in the world* for a while, something would trigger a memory and send our brains back to Vietnam. Sometimes, out in the field, set up for the night, I would be talking to a fellow soldier and all of a sudden see blood streaming down his face. Dead, shot in the head by a sniper. Death in an instant, these memories come up in your head years later when you are trying to maintain some kind of life with your family. PTSD follows you and if you don't find some way to deal with it, it will ruin your life or kill you. Many combat Veterans die from suicide, and a few times I have had those thoughts. As I am writing in my home office, that date of July 7th is looming. As I remember these things and write about them, tears are in my eyes. All I can think about is that the enemy was everywhere, our guys lying dead and wounded on the ground, and enemy soldiers dead in front of our weapons. The loss of friends and fellow soldiers never leaves your memories. Every year I call my friend Bill Dillehay in Florida, or he calls me, to see how we are doing on that July date 53 years later. He was part of my 7 man squad that day. I still see images of the men we lost, and others that were wounded or died later.

Many times as I walked through the jungle, I would think to myself *what the FUCK am I doing here* and of course the famous resolve *I am not going to die here*. I would look up at any passenger jet flying by and assume that it was going home. *How can I get in one and get out of here?* You know the song by the Animals *We gotta get out of this place, if it's the last thing we ever do*. It was one of our favorite songs over there.

I thought that my involvement with Vietnam was over, when in fact my experiences and the resulting PTSD would always be with me. This should have been the beginning of my life as a civilian. I was in great shape physically but did not realize how much I had been affected by what had happened over there and by the things I had seen. One morning my mother came into my room to wake me and tell me that she and my father were going out. Well, that was the last time she ever did that. I jumped up, grabbed her by the throat, knocked her down and got on top of her. Luckily, I realized in a few seconds that I was home in my bedroom and no longer in the jungles of Vietnam. They just sent us home with no thought to how we would adjust or how we would deal with the memories. There was no deprogramming to help us rejoin civilian life. I began receiving my 10% disability from the VA, which in 1969 was $23 a month.

It was time for me to move forward and get a real civilian job. My father was still working for the New York Central Railroad and had become a payroll master by the time I graduated from high school. At the time, he had gotten me a good job there as an insurance clerk, which lasted for about six months until I was drafted. After my discharge, I again went to work for the railroad, this time as a switchman, working at an elevated station on 125th Street in Harlem. It was like controlling toy trains. I had a big, lighted board in front of me showing where all the trains were coming into New York City on their way to Grand Central Terminal in Manhattan. I was good at it and my pay was $90 a week, not bad for 1968. Gas was 29 cents a gallon. That command post was above the street with stairs leading up to it, right in the middle of the Harlem drug trade area. It was very easy for me to get anything I wanted, all I had to do was walk down the stairs. Pot was always available, LSD was becoming popular, uppers and downers were easy to get. That railroad job was not for me, I was too restless from my experiences. I resigned and began looking for something else. I started spending time with my old friends, some of whom had gotten heavily involved with drugs while I was away. I started using heroin and selling drugs.

My good friend John from high school, with his partner, had started a company manufacturing and selling pipes for smoking hash and pot. They invented the hash pipe belt buckle. In the 60s and 70s, fashionable drug paraphernalia was very popular and was sold in what we called head shops. This was my first sales position on the road and my territory was from Miami to Boston. I would fill up my car with pipes and other drug related items and do mostly a cash business with retail stores. I did well but it was a tough time for me, drugs were available everywhere I went. I was arrested several times for drug related offenses, and was eventually formally charged and had to appear in court. My father got me an Italian lawyer and we went in front of an Italian judge. I got suspended sentences, and there were fines and probation for this first offense. My drug use kept getting worse, it was an easy way to forget all the horrors of Vietnam. When you kill someone, even to save your own life in combat, it changes you forever. I left that job selling drug paraphernalia. This cut me off from my old friend John for many years.

I became involved with a group that was selling pot. We had great connections for kilos of very good Mexican marijuana. We did business out of a motel on Route 46 in South Hackensack, NJ and would take the customer there to complete the transaction. If a transaction did not go well, we would just take their money, throw them out and move to a different room. My drug habit was getting worse. I left that group doing business at the motel.

My next job was at the Landlubber Jeans warehouse, and I started stealing merchandise to sell on the side to cover my habit and got caught. My father was there for me again, he got me the same lawyer and we went before the same judge. I was sentenced to a year in the Bergen County Jail, so off I went and they put me on a 21 day methadone detox. That didn't work well, and I was sick for weeks as a result of that treatment. After

I was there for about 90 days, my father worked something out with the judge and got me released. I was a mess at 22 years old, living at home with my parents, had no car, no money, and just enough for bus fare to get around.

Before I went to jail I had been seeing a girl named Laura, and she had visited me there a few times. She let me use her car to get a job so that I could make enough money to buy my own car and that is exactly what I did. I don't even remember all the jobs, I was still using drugs so my memory is clouded. I bought a new AMC Hornet, gave Laura back her car and she moved on. I dated a lot of girls but nothing was serious. My life was going nowhere. I went from job to job, spent hours in bars at night, and my drug use got worse and worse.

In 1971 my parents sold their house and moved to Bayville, NJ, about 60 miles south of Teaneck, on the eastern shore of New Jersey. I stayed in northern New Jersey, and started working for a company in Hackensack selling advertising space in newspapers and magazines over the phone, and met my friend Bobby there. He was a Navy Vet who had been stationed on an aircraft carrier in Vietnam, and we got an apartment together in Englewood. I did well there and made pretty good money. The company promoted me to training manager, gave me a raise, and after a few weeks they flew me out to their headquarters in Idaho to meet with management. They put me up at a hotel for the night, and the next day when I went into the office they fired me, and gave me my last paycheck and a ticket home. I could not understand what had happened and no one would tell me. I flew home and went directly to their office in Hackensack. Everything was gone, furniture, desk phones and office equipment. I found out later that day that they were under indictment for fraud and were closed down for good. The indictment was federal and luckily I was not involved. I already had a police record.

The memories of combat kept invading my brain and the drug use got worse, but I still didn't understand anything about PTSD. I would wake up in the middle of the night thinking I had fallen asleep on ambush. The images of the men I had killed in combat and ambushes were in my dreams. Sometimes I would just cry not knowing why, and holidays were depressing. I still did not know why this was happening, and of course by this time we all knew about Agent Orange. A lot of Veterans were already suffering the effects. So, in addition to the flashbacks of war, the threat of getting sick from Agent Orange exposure was hanging over me and still is. It seemed that the government was trying to cover that up by ignoring the problem, and there was not much help for Veterans. Only drugs made my life tolerable.

We knew that in South Vietnam there were revenge squads that went after South Vietnamese civilians and soldiers who were resisting the North Vietnamese Communist Party. They tortured them for information, then either killed or imprisoned them. After a while, I began to imagine that hit squads were coming after me in the United States. I had trouble sleeping and was always watching my back. I know it sounds crazy, but I had seen this happening over there and could not shake the feeling. That fear was part of my mindset while trying to get back to a regular life.

Then one night I met my future wife in a bar in Bogota, NJ. She was sitting at a table with her girlfriend having drinks over a bowl of potato chips. I walked over, grabbed a chip and sat down. Funny thing is her girlfriend from that night is my writing collaborator in this book. A little over a year later I married the girl with the potato chips. Right at the time of me writing this book we will have been married 50 years. We were immediately attracted to each other but Sandy didn't think I was good for her and dragged her out of the bar, but not before she stuck a napkin in my hand with her phone number. Kathy was very slender and was wearing a low cut top with plenty of cleavage showing. She was beautiful. I had met my life partner.

My drug habit made life much harder than it should have been, but my relationship with Kathy was going well, even with all my problems. She was 22 at the time, had a 5 year old son from a previous situation, and had very recently moved out of her parent's home and into an apartment in Englewood. I moved in with her, but continued to pay my share of the rent on the other apartment until Bobby found another roommate. That was added financial pressure for a while. My drug use had a life of its own. I was doing heroin every day, my problems were a part of our lives. Kathy and I got engaged. I was an addict, and she knew about it and was committed to helping me. I decided to go on a methadone maintenance program as an outpatient at a facility in New York City. What a horror that turned out to be, as they increased my dosage to 120 milligrams per day. It turned me into a zombie, but at least my PTSD symptoms were kept in check with these legal and illegal drugs. At one point I was selling some of the methadone to buy other drugs. I started having car accidents. We got married in September 1974, had a small wedding and reception, and went to the Playboy Club in North Jersey for our honeymoon. I was strung out the whole time.

I floundered around at several sales jobs that were going nowhere, but I earned enough money on and off to support us while my wife went to drafting school. She got a good job with a local company in Fort Lee, NJ and we managed. I got a job selling furniture with Reliable Furniture in Hackensack. Up until then I had hated working, but selling furniture seemed right for me. By 1976, Kathy was pregnant and we were looking for a house. She researched an ad for Veterans to get a VA loan with the GI Bill with no down payment. The baby was due in January 1977 so we had to find something. The application process was lengthy, but like many things that we had to do, we never gave up. Eventually, after a long day in Newark with my six month pregnant wife, a major in the office noticed that I was a Vietnam Combat Veteran, and got our papers processed. We put down a $10 deposit on a $51,999 house in Passaic County, NJ, and had just enough to cover closing costs. We moved in on Halloween, and Kathy was ready with candy for the neighborhood children. She had to leave her job because the drive would now be longer, and the baby was due soon. We had a nice house in a beautiful neighborhood, and I was doing well selling furniture.

In late 1977, on my own, I stopped drugs completely. It took me two years from beginning to end, and I was sick on and off during the second year with chills and shakes, but I did it. I was 28 years old and have never done another drug to this day. I do not take pain medication and still refuse Novocaine for dental work. Our son was born in 1977, and 22 months later our daughter was born. Along with the son my wife already had, we now had three kids.

I was still drinking and started gambling a lot more. Gambling had begun to take the place of drugs in my life, although I did not realize it at the time. Meanwhile, in spite of that, my career was advancing. Reliable Furniture transferred me to a larger, newer store. My sales record at the new store got better and better and my pay was straight commission. I was steadily making more than I had at the other store, and management was noticing. Kathy also worked during this time tending bar at night and working coat check concessions in restaurants. I watched the kids at night when she worked. I quit smoking completely.

By the time I was 32 years old I was doing very well in the furniture business and I managed, even with all my problems, to provide for my family and we did alright. My wife still worked nights in restaurants so we had two incomes with which to pay bills. I stayed with Reliable Furniture Company, and after a while they promoted me to manager of a failing store on Route 18 in East Brunswick, NJ. When I started there, the store was disorganized and the employees lacked direction. It was a large store with two floors, and I took it from $40,000 a month to $120,000 a month in three months. Every store I managed for the company did better when I ran it and I made good money.

I was making a name for myself in the furniture business and we were able to catch up financially. It was also the beginning of learning about how my time in the service had affected me. The pressure finally got to me and I had my first daytime attack. I was with a customer who was looking at a rug, and when I bent down to check the price tag, I got dizzy and could not stand back up. My heart started palpitating. Ten years after my discharge and this new horror was happening. Until then it was dreams waking me up at night and occasional flashbacks to scenes in the jungle, but nothing like this. The flashbacks and panic attacks became more frequent and more severe over the next few years. Trying to deal with the dizziness and heart palpitations during the day at work, and not being able to sleep at night, was what I was living with. I had no idea what was causing this and called it *Disdain Brisbain*. I felt awful, and yet my career in the furniture business was more and more successful. I was desperate enough at this point to think that my hour and a half ride each way was part of the problem. On an impulse I bought a new Cadillac, which we couldn't afford, hoping that the smooth ride would help. It did not. I sold the car a year later.

Soon they gave me a bigger store to manage, and then their biggest and best store in Paramus. I was making even more money but feeling worse and worse. I had become good friends with Bobby, another very successful Reliable Furniture manager, and we decided to go into business together and open our own stores. This is not the same Bobby that I had shared an apartment with when I was single. He and his wife stayed with us for a few weeks while the business was being set up and they were looking for a house. We called our new company Today's Furniture.

Running this new business kept me very busy, which I initially thought was good for me at the time. We opened three stores in New Jersey, in Lodi, Jersey City, and Fairfield. The Fairfield store was in a more upscale area than the other two, so we carried some more expensive, better brands of furniture at that location. One day, one of my salesmen had a customer who was furnishing a new house, and it looked like he would be buying a lot of pieces. He was Asian and spoke with an accent. Aside from being one of the owners, I would often assume the position of store manager for the day at any location. Customers expected and deserved a discount if they were buying several pieces. I would always have my salesman set the customer up for a takeover with a manager at the end for the price drop, and to confirm the order. This customer had chosen a lot of pieces and I had negotiated a nice price drop for him, including delivery and set-up. It just so happened that I was wearing one of my Vietnam Veteran shirts that day. He said to me, "So you're a Vietnam Veteran?" I said yes to that and he told me that he was also a Vietnam Veteran, so I asked him exactly where and what branch of military. He said, "I was mostly in the north. I was a general in the North Vietnamese Army." I never expected to hear something like that. The enemy was right here in my store, but it was 1985 and the war was long over. It was a chilling feeling and we did not continue the conversation. He handed me his credit card to cover everything, and we scheduled the delivery. I assume he was pleased with the merchandise, I never saw him again.

Business was great but Bobby and I had a lot of conflicts, and eventually he bought my share of the business and brought in his brother to take my place. At the time I was disappointed, but later came to realize that I was better off without that added responsibility and stress. They could not manage the business without me and the company went under, and somehow Bobby lost his house. I had already gone back to working in other furniture stores and, as always, did very well.

Although I was finished with drugs, I was still soothing my symptoms with alcohol and gambling. I participated in sports betting with bookies, played local private poker games, and started going to casinos in Atlantic City. That was the bomb, black jack, roulette, slots, craps. I kept on losing money. Kathy had been aware of my previous drug use and current alcohol problems, but gambling was very easy to hide from her. Although I wasn't suffering dizzy spells and palpitations so much anymore, I knew something was still very wrong.

I started going to doctors and they sent me for a lot of tests, upper and lower GI, blood tests, heart tests, nothing showed up. Physically I was healthy. One day I went to the VA in Newark looking for medical information and I mistakenly went into the Marine recruiting office. After talking to the officer in charge about my problems, he recognized my symptoms and told me I was suffering from PTSD. This was before I had identified myself as a Vietnam Combat Veteran. I signed up at a local Vet center and this was when I really began to understand my problems. I started having one-on-one therapy with a psychologist who had experienced combat as a captain in the Army in Iraq. The first thing I learned was that fighting the symptoms only made them worse, but working with what I was feeling was hard, too. I began to understand that it would get worse before it got better. A lot of Vietnam Vets did not want to talk about what was happening to them, but talking about it is the only way to move forward. The VA recognized my condition and, along with treating me, increased my disability level along with my VA benefit. Getting a higher percentage of course meant more money, but just as importantly, it meant recognition of my service to my country. A lot of the things you do in combat are necessary to stay alive, but they stay in your memories. When I was sent to Vietnam I was only 19.

Kathy was still working during these years, and we managed to support ourselves. I started my stint at Gamblers Anonymous to try and stop my gambling addiction. This was difficult because I never really thought of my gambling as an addiction, for me it was self medication to suppress my PTSD symptoms. I hated GA, it was the worst ever for me, it is called a program because it programs you. I saw what it did to other people and I did not want that for myself. I was miserable and quit after being in it for 10 years. Back then it looked like I would be working the rest of my life, since Kathy and I had accumulated some debt as a result of my gambling.

I still worked in furniture stores and was always near the top in sales. My PTSD was still coming on strong but I was learning how to cope with the dreadful symptoms instead of struggling with them. Sometimes at night, when it was at its worst, I would take a shower, which seemed to calm it down. I let go of the fight and began to feel better after the first six months of therapy at the Vet center. The physical symptoms began to fade away. I still had dreams, but in time they were not so severe. I still have the same therapist I started with around 2009. That is when I filed the paperwork to try and get a larger percentage of disability from the VA. With my therapist Jonathan's help, I got to 50% by 2010. I was still working at the time, selling mattresses at Sleepy's, and never dreamed that it would be my last job.

In 2012, I got my 100% disability from the VA and also began collecting my Social Security. In New Jersey, as well as in some other states, for a combat Veteran with boots-on-the-ground combat designation, the property tax on his residence is waived and I qualified. Now I could retire and have enough income for Kathy and I to begin paying off our debts and live comfortably. All three kids were on their own and doing well. In 2012 my wife and I bought our first camper. I attached it to our Jeep Liberty and we went on a three month trip out west to visit my sister and her family in Wyoming. Then we went on to Yellowstone and states to the north and saw many wonderful things in our beautiful country.

Today is July 4th, 2021 and I am preparing another package of notes for Sandy. The memory of what happened 54 years ago on July 7, 1967 always floods my mind this time of year. From that event, of our two squads, of the men that I kept in touch with, the only three still alive that I know about are

Bill Dillehay, Vinny and me. That infamous day our camp was overrun was the worst day of my life. The memory always haunted me, but I never consciously associated it with a date. I couldn't understand why, around the week of July 7th every year, I would always feel uneasy and shaken, and have heart palpitations, dizzy spells and just bad feelings. In 2011 my wife and I went to the Army archives in Maryland and looked up a lot of things about my time in the service and about that event. It took a week of studying different accounts of my unit, the 4th of the 23rd, 25th Infantry Division, to find that battle. It was horrible to read about all that carnage and the documented communications (see Appendix III). When I started going to my Company C reunions after 2012, and started talking to other men about that day, some of them did not remember the date but they all remembered the event.

When I speak to my friend Bill Dillehay, we talk about that event in 1967. For years, like me, he suffered anxiety and could not sleep during that week and did not know why. He also did not associate a date with that event but somehow inside himself, like me, he knew. My research was helpful to both of us. I shared with him copies of the radio conversations between our unit and base camp of what was happening to us, and they are haunting. We didn't have time to be scared, we were just trying to kill as many of them as possible to stop them from killing us. Bill is 100% disabled from Agent Orange complications and PTSD, and as of 2024, still lives in Florida on a 50 acre ranch. His property is like a Vietnam War Museum. He has a room that looks exactly like one of our hooches, with everything just like it was in Cu Chi Base Camp, along with a lot of Army paraphernalia. He owns several Army Jeeps from that era and a deuce and a half-truck (a special military cargo truck) with a 50 caliber inoperable machine gun on top. They all run. His mind has never left there. He has a vintage Harley-Davidson and a classic Corvette in a garage near the back of the property. Every other car or truck he has ever owned is still on the property, left to rust wherever they stopped running. They are not cared for like his Vietnam vehicles. He is my dear friend and we talk all the time on the phone and used to see each other at reunions. My wife and I spend time in Florida every year with our camper, and he created a spot on his ranch for us to park with water, electric and sewer hook-ups. We can stay for a week at a time with him. Kathy took this picture of us in 2024 when the four of us went out together (picture 40). He is very sick with Triple Play from Agent Orange exposure, cancer, heart disease and diabetes. He struggles with the help of his wonderful wife Jane, who is a nurse. I took this picture of them during that same visit (picture 41). He maintains his life but I see it gets tougher and tougher all the time. Bill became a cameraman for ESPN and earned several Emmys for his fine work. He even went to Cuba in the 1970s to film baseball games. May God bless him. Kathy and I love him and his wife. As of May 2024, he is still alive.

Dennis Reilly and I have stayed in touch all these years. He lives with his longtime girlfriend, Monica, in San Antonio, TX. Kathy and I were able to visit him in 2021. He also has been suffering for years from the effects of Agent Orange, has advanced diabetes, his kidneys are failing and he is on dialysis.

He faces these issues bravely, is cheerful whenever we see him, and goes on with his life as best as he can. He and Monica were able to go out to lunch with us during that visit (picture 42), and we took a walk along the beautiful San Antonio River Walk near where they live. He used to travel around the US to Veterans gatherings, which is where I would often see him. Those traveling days are over for him.

Frank Chiorazzi was a friend from high school. He was a year older than me, joined the Marines after graduation, and was sent to Vietnam. Before we were drafted we would play pool at the Family Billiards Lounge in Bergenfield, and at night a group of us would sing acapella outside of the pool hall. We would go off to clubs in New York State because the drinking age there was still 18. This was common for kids from North Jersey. My parents and his parents knew each other and kept in touch while we were in the service, they were members of Saint Anastasia Catholic Church. He was as good a guy as could be and was always ready to help everyone and anyone. He made it through Vietnam, a Marine in combat in the demilitarized zone, but like all of us, he was exposed to Agent Orange. When he came home, like me, he felt the effects of PTSD, had a lot of dead-end jobs, but never married. I know he drank a lot and smoked pot. He still went to play pool at the Family Billiards Lounge and eventually took over running it. I used to visit him there all the time to talk and one day when I came in, he looked awful and told me he wasn't feeling well. About three weeks later, I got a call from a friend telling me that he had died from one of the Triple Play cancers. I went to the wake, church service and burial, and a lot of our high school friends were there. It was so sad, his brother was devastated. Their parents had passed on years before. It was a sorrowful day for another Vietnam Veteran and his friends and family left behind.

My friend Eddie M***** was a Vietnam Marine Veteran who lived about a mile from us in Passaic County. We met around 2011 when we were both at a Memorial Day event honoring Veterans and started talking because we were both wearing Vietnam Veteran hats. At this time I had already begun helping other Vets get their PTSD and Agent Orange disability benefits. Eddie became my next case. Among his other health problems, he had developed bladder cancer, had to have his bladder removed, and for a few years had been using a catheter just to pee. After we got him involved with the VA, the amazing surgeons there removed part of his colon and used that to make a new bladder for him. I learned that he had a severely handicapped son. I know several Vets who had been exposed to that Agent Orange poison who later had children with serious problems. After we sent in his papers he got 50% disability, and after a few years got to 100%. He was the first one in his town to get the 100% disability status, which he and his family needed and deserved. It is my mission in life to help get Vietnam Combat Veterans to 100% disability to help them live comfortably. We both go to therapy at the Oakland Vet Center for one-on-one sessions with a therapist, and we have group meetings as well. As of May 2024, he is still alive.

As I continued with therapy, I met a marine I'll call Dave at the East Orange VA medical facility. We talked about our experiences, PTSD and therapy, and what I had learned about treatments and benefits for Combat Veterans. One day he lifted his shirt and showed me five black marks on his torso, and he told me his story. During a firefight, his unit had been overrun by the North Vietnamese and many of his fellow marines were dead or wounded. As the NVA came through they stabbed men lying on the ground with bayonets and he had to lie down next to dead soldiers and play dead. He was stabbed 5 times and stayed perfectly still. They missed all his vital organs and he lived. My God, I don't know how he did it. I saw him a few more times at meetings and lost track of him. I never learned his last name or where he lived.

Once I got past the point of knowing what PTSD is, then I had to learn how to deal with it in everyday life. I learned to get the heart palpitations to slowly stop by not trying to stop them. The panic attacks can manifest themselves in other ways, too. Sometimes there are feelings of inadequacy and thoughts of suicide or impending death. It always finds ways to come at you and you have to deflect it. Most of my care for PTSD has been at my local Vet Center in individual therapy or group therapy with other veterans.

When I go into a flashback it can last a while, nothing I know of can describe it. It can be so easily triggered, lots of things can set you off, like old songs from that era. Music from artists like The Temptations or The Four Tops will do it, especially *Tell It Like It Is* by Aaron Neville. When I relax now at night and remember the things I saw over there, and the things I had to do to survive, the words of a Jimmy Hendrix song come to mind.

The song is *All Along the Watchtower* and the words are "and life is but a joke." Now that I am older I think *what was it all for?*

Another thing that sets me off is the smell of tar. They would spread tar on the roads in Vietnam when it was very hot and dry to keep the sand from flying around. Anything that sounds like bombs or gunfire can do it. I can't go on a plane, train or in an elevator. I can't go in an MRI, even an open MRI, I start panicking. Memories that come back to you out of the blue, being in tight, dark places, remind me of the tunnels. This can be so real that you can't escape the thoughts. These feelings are still with me, but I know what places and situations to avoid. Hallucinations and nightmares are common. Crowds are impossible to be in. I live with the fear that all that exposure to Agent Orange years ago will still make me sick.

After the training I received in the service, learning some hand-to-hand combat techniques, I know how to kill someone without a weapon. When I first came back I was 130 pounds, so I might have looked like an easy target but I was not. I can handle myself very well, not as well now that I am going on 75, but I am sure I can still do ok. Sometimes things happen and I perceive a threat from someone just because he is there and I immediately size him up. I look for weak spots, am always ready, and usually for nothing. When I get angry or feel threatened my adrenaline starts pumping and I am dangerous and vulnerable at the same time. I know to never go after anyone in traffic after they do something stupid on the road. My therapist at the Vet Center helps me keep anger in check. I fall apart sometimes and have to find something or someone to help me come back to reality. I often call my daughter, she understands my situation and she can get me to calm down from an attack. I'm usually crying by the time I call her.

The struggle with PTSD will always be a part of my life. It affects every soldier's life as a result of traumatic experiences left over from combat. After Vietnam, battle weary soldiers were treated badly, usually by people in charge that were never in battle. Does the government help soldiers with PTSD and Agent Orange issues? It tries now but still falls short a lot of the time. I run into a lot of Veterans all the time, many still suffering from those experiences and many with the Triple Play, diabetes, cancer, heart disease. We easily identify each other since most of us wear Vietnam Veteran hats and t-shirts. I have helped a lot of them with problems from exposure to Agent Orange, all of which have to be documented with facts to qualify for benefits. Where it happened, how it happened, who it happened to and how it affected you must be documented. I learned a lot about what is available for veterans and I find it therapeutic to help others. Problems from Agent Orange are much harder to prove, even if you have all the diseases they would only give 30% - 50%. In 2020, new legislation was enacted to expand the VA's list of medical conditions associated with Agent Orange to include bladder cancer, hypothyroidism and Parkinson's Disease. Why our government did not face this problem early on and help our soldiers who were affected, I don't know.

These are the experiences of an ordinary young man from New Jersey put in an extraordinary position, in an unwelcomed war. I have to thank my wonderful wife for putting up with me through the years. She stood beside me through thick and thin, and believe me there was a lot of thin. I thank my extraordinary children, Chuck, Keith and Nicole, for supporting me during some very difficult times. Our family has grown over the years and is still growing. We have six grandchildren and one great-grandchild and we often take them on special camping trips with us. Abigail, Cameron, Nicholas and Vinessa are the perfect ages to go on camping trips and to concerts and festivals with us. Sometimes I take them fishing on the boats that go out of our Jersey Shore marinas. Rae Ann is our great-granddaughter, and her mother is our granddaughter, Melanie. She is seven and enjoys the park and going to the movies with me. Our youngest grandson is Guy, born in 2024. May God bless my parents, Nick and Betty, who had to put up with me and my problems after I came home. They were always there to help, and never gave up on me. I am grateful to my wife's best friend, Sandy, who is also my good friend, for spending so much time on this work. And thank you to the many other Vietnam Veterans with whom I have had difficult conversations over the years, giving me even more inspiration to write this book.

It is February 2021 and we have a new, larger camper that I pull with my pickup truck. It has a big slide-out to open up the kitchen area and we can cook outside. It is the only way I can travel. I cannot be in a train or plane. If we are in a restaurant, I have to sit facing the door. I have two sweet-tempered Shih-Tzu service dogs, Rosie and Tulip, that help me remain calm and grounded. We take them almost everywhere. My other two Shih-Tzus, Daisy and Lilly, are in Service Dog Heaven. It is 2022, I am in my house in Passaic County, NJ, working on the last notes for this book and will send the package to Sandy before Kathy and I leave for another trip.

TO MY FELLOW VETERANS

My greatest passion is helping other Vietnam Veterans. I work with Vietnam Veterans of America, a great organization that has done wonders for Veterans who need and deserve disability. A lot of Veterans do not know all the benefits they are entitled to, so I always have my Vietnam Veterans hat on and look for guys with the same and connect with them. I have helped many Vietnam Veterans get 100% disability which gives them around $3,850 a month for life tax free. After serving their country, many suffer from PTSD, depression and the effects of Agent Orange.

Property tax in New Jersey and some other states is waived for some Combat Veterans.

There are Vets who qualify but do not believe they deserve it. There are a lot of homeless Vietnam Veterans. Many have tried to get help, had difficulties with the application process and gave up. I learned from my buddy and fellow Vietnam Veteran Frank

Mezzadri what is necessary to be included in your application for disability and I pass it on.

A percentage of the royalties from this book will be donated to Homeless Veterans groups so more Veterans and their families can get help.

Local Vet Centers can be found at 877-927-8387

Contact information for Richie is on our website.

More information for Veterans is on our website www.lessthanahero.com

You can reach out to us at lessthanahero@aol.com

APPENDIX I

:WARK EVENING NEWS, FRIDAY, AUGUST 11, 1967

Staff Photo by Slavin

HEADING DOWN—Sgt. Richard Monteleone of Teaneck watches fellow "tunnel rat" Pfc. Gregory Iezzi of Jersey City squeeze into a Viet Cong tunnel entrance.

Please go to our website to read
this page of the 1967 article.

www.lessthanahero.com

APPENDIX II

Herbert Sherrill

PERSONAL DATA:
  Home of Record: St Albans, NY
  Date of birth: 10/03/1946
MILITARY DATA:
  Service Branch: Army of the United States
  Grade at loss: E5
  Rank: Sergeant
Promotion Note: None
  ID No: 12695908
  MOS: 11B40: Infantryman
  Length Service: 03
  Unit: C CO, 4TH BN, 23RD INFANTRY, 25TH INF
                  DIV, USARV
CASUALTY DATA:
  Start Tour: 08/25/1966
  Incident Date: 06/29/1967
  Casualty Date: 06/29/1967
  Status Date: Not Applicable
  Status Change: Not Applicable
  Age at Loss: 20
  Location: Binh Duong Province, South Vietnam
  Remains: Body recovered
  Repatriated: Not Applicable
  Identified: Not Applicable
  Casualty Type: Hostile, died outright
  Casualty Reason: Ground casualty
  Casualty Detail: Multiple fragmentation wounds
  URL: https://www.VirtualWall.org/ds/SherrillHx01a.htm
  Data accessed: 9/24/2024

APPENDIX III

CONFIDENTIAL   51   X 0/???

DAILY STAFF DUTY OFFICER'S LOG				PAGE NO. 1		NO. OF PAGES	

ORGANIZATION OR INSTALLATION	PERIOD COVERED			
S2/S3 1st Bde 25th Inf Div	FROM		TO	
	HOUR 0001	DATE 7 Jul 67	HOUR 2400	DATE 7 Jul 67

ITEM NO.	TIME IN	TIME OUT	INCIDENTS, MESSAGES, ORDERS, ETC.	ACTION TAKEN	INI- TIALS
1	0001		Journal Opened		
2	0034		Late Entry (SGT Harrison) 0028 Bunker 5 two people were badly burned by WP grenade, TOC is sending a doctor & ambulance to bunker 5 at this time, reason for accident unk 2-14 rear		
3	0005		Have neg commo w/Viking Lima, G3 SGT Gallin- lime will contact CU CHI Subsector	G3	
4	0200		1st Bde Sitrep N/C	G3	
5	0300		1st Bde Sitrep N/C	G3	
22	0400		1st Bde Sitrep N/C	G3	
7	0425		Late Entry 0415: C 4-23 receiving mortar fire at this time, also arty firing Defcons	G3	
8	0458		Recap of mortar & RPG-2 attack of C 4-23, attack started approx 0415, mortars & RPG-2 came from vic XT630200 unk VC force, unk nr of mortar & RPG-2 rds. 5 WIA litter, 4 WIA amb, 1 KIA. VC broke contact of mortar & RPG-2 fire at approx 0435, dust off at RON psns at 0503, 0510 dust off can't land at this time, a track is burning & exploded. 1st dust off on ground 0537	G3	
??	0605		C 4-23 (as of this time) 5 KIA, 16 WIA (10	G3	

TYPED NAME AND GRADE OF OFFICER OR OFFICIAL ON DUTY
FRANK M. WROBLEWSKI, CPT, Inf

SIGNATURE

DA FORM 1594
1 NOV 62

CONFIDENTIAL

C-149-36-3.314

PPC-Japan

ITEM NO.	TIME IN	TIME OUT	INCIDENTS, MESSAGES, ORDERS, ETC.	ACTION TAKEN	INI-TIALS
			amb, 6 litter) one track completely dest		
			Ref Item 7		
10	0630		Ref Item 7: 24 WIA, 5 KIA 1 track completely	G3	
			dest, 3 other tracks disabled. Unit also rec		
			SA fire during the attack		
11	0700		Recon 4-9 started road clearing to TRANG BANG	G3	
12	0720		Sct Plt 4-23 departed Camp CU CHI to secure		
			engr work vic XT615167		
13	0750		C 4-9 1st lift off PZ at 0731H, 2d lift off	G3	
			PZ at 0743H LZ is vic CU CHI		
22	0815		B 4-23 & engr started movement from CU CHI		
			to vic XT7019		
15	0755		C 4-9 3d lift off PZ LZ vic CU CHI		
16	0820		I 4-23 departed RON for TRUNG LAP to secure		
			4.2 plat to CU CHI		
17	0825		B 4-9 1st lift off PZ LZ vic CU CHI		
18	0845		C 4-9 1st lift completed 0750H, 2d lift com-	G3	
			pleted 0805H, 3d lift completed 0815H, B 4-9		
			1st lift completed 0835		
19	0940		4-9 reports Co B 1st lift off Co base at 0820	G3	
			hrs, on ground 0835 hrs; 2d lift off ground		
			0840H, on ground CU CHI 0853; 3d lift off		
20			0845, on ground CU CHI 0858, KHIEM HANH RF		

		DAILY STAFF OFFICER'S LOG		PAGE NO. 3	NO. OF PAGES
ORGANIZATION OR INSTALLATION				PERIOD COVERED	

	HOUR	DATE	HOUR	DATE
FROM	0001	7 Jul 67		
TO			2400	7 Jul 67

ITEM NO.	TIME IN	TIME OUT	INCIDENTS, MESSAGES, ORDERS, ETC.	ACTION TAKEN	INITIALS
			have spotted VC plat vic XT480305, req permission from 4-9 to engage, permission granted		
20	0950		4-23 Inf reports that at 0800 Sct plt linked up w/engr and began security ops vic XT615167 Co B and engr are working vic XT6917. Co's A & C are sweeping north from vic XT571198 and XT622203 departing at 0905 and 0907 respectively	03	
21	0950		B 4-23 1 track det 1 AT mine vic XT700180, 3 litter track was turned over dust off req at 0955H	03	
22	1005		A 4-9 1st lift off PZ 0906, completed at CU CHI at 0917H. 2d lift off PZ 0910, completed 0921H. 3d lift off PZ 0932H, completed 0950. 1 plat A 4-9 off PZ 0906H for C 4-23 loc, completed 0919	03	
23	1015		B 4-23 dust off complete for 3 WIA	03	
24	1020		Late Entry: 2-14 Sitrep N/G 1000 hrs	03	
25	1030		B 4-23 Ref Item 21 this log: Mine was believed to be all powder in excess of 100 lbs left crater 6 ft deep 12 ft wide hit track right front turned track over on its top track total loss	03	
26	1040		4-9 reports the advisor from BAO DON sighted	03	

TYPED NAME AND GRADE OF OFFICER OR OFFICIAL ON DUTY   SIGNATURE

DA FORM 1594
1 NOV 62   PREVIOUS EDITION OF THIS FORM IS OBSOLETE.   FFC-Japan

www.ingramcontent.com/pod-product-compliance
Lightning Source LLC
Chambersburg PA
CBHW051150120626
46547CB00012B/1027